Mark Phillip Smith

Lake Malawi Cichlids

Everything About History, Setting Up an Aquarium, Health Concerns, and Spawning

Filled with Full-color Photographs

Illustrations by Michele Earle-Bridges

BARRON'S

2 CONTENTS

Introduction 5

Diversity of Cichlids 5

Two Categories of Cichlids 6

General Information
about Cichlids 6

The History of
Lake Malawi 9

General Facts about
Lake Malawi 12

What are Cichlids? 12

**Setting Up Your
Aquarium** 15

Aquarium Size and Shape 15

The Aquarium Stand 16

Types of Filtration 16

Aquarium Water
Chemistry 19

Heater and Thermometer 19

Lighting 20

Decorations 20

Sand/Gravel 21

Live Plants 21

HOW-TO: Learning about
Filters 22

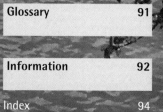

Maintaining the Aquarium   25

Water Changes   25

Diet   27

Parasites and Bacterial Infections   27

Quarantine and the Hospital Aquarium   30

Adding New Malawi Cichlids to an Established Aquarium   31

Spawning Tips for Lake Malawi Cichlids   33

Setting the Groundwork   33

Difficult-to-Spawn Species   34

Raising Juvenile Malawi Cichlids   36

HOW-TO: Separation from Parents   38

A Representative Selection of Lake Malawi Cichlids   41

The Mbuna Group   42

The Haplochromis Group   63

Glossary   91

Information   92

Index   94

INTRODUCTION

Diversity of Cichlids

Of the nine families of fishes represented in Lake Malawi, one family that overshadows all others in terms of numbers and diversity is the family Cichlidae. On the African continent, this family is represented throughout most river systems and especially in all the great lakes of Africa. The cichlids of Lake Malawi have colonized and evolved into a vast array of endemic species, making it the greatest repository of cichlid species in all of Africa. The cichlids constitute approximately 85 percent of the total number of fish species in the lake, and in terms of total numbers of species—cichlids and non-cichlids alike—Lake Malawi contains more species than any other lake on earth. Current estimates place the number of cichlid species, including those formally described by science as well as those recognized as new, at approximately 800! Ichthyologists have gotten around to describing only about 300 species, leaving some 500 species yet to be described.

There are two categories of cichlids found in Lake Malawi: the Haplochromines and the Tilapiines. The Haplochromines dominate and contain over 99 percent of the lake's cichlid fauna, while the Tilapiines make up five species. The Haplochromines are broken down into three

Sandy shore at Likoma Island. Sandy areas of the lake help to act as barriers to many species from the Mbuna group. Most species from the Haplochromis group tend to be found predominantly in this habitat.

groups: the Astatotilapia group, the Haplochromis group, and the Mbuna group. The Astatotilapia group contains a single nonendemic species, *A. calliptera,* and is related to the cichlids of Lakes Victoria, Edward, George, Kyoga, and Kivu. The Haplochromis group, endemic to Lake Malawi, consists of species that are predominantly open water or sand dwelling in their habitat preference. As juveniles, they possess a silvery coloration and ill-defined egg spots on the anal fin. Finally, the Mbuna group, also endemic to the lake, consists of species that are predominantly rock dwelling in their habitat preference. They possess juvenile coloration that is blue, yellow, or brown, and usually have clearly defined egg spots on the anal fin.

The other category of cichlids found in Lake Malawi are the Tilapiines. The Tilapiines can be further broken down into two groups: the mouthbrooders and the substrate spawners. The subgenus name *Nyasalapia* is frequently given to encompass the endemic species flock of three very closely related *Oreochromis* species of the first group. There is some controversy regarding the usage of this subgenus name, but it makes for a convenient label to distinguish the three endemic species from the rest. *Oreochromis shiranus* also belongs to this first group. *Tilapia rendalli* is the only representative that belongs to the second group, as it is a substrate spawner. These latter two species, while regular inhabitants of the lake, are not endemic, and are found elsewhere throughout southern and eastern Africa.

Two Categories of Cichlids

I. The Haplochromines
A. Astatotilapia Group
Astatotilapia

B. Haplochromis Group
Altiocorpus
Aristochromis
Aulonocara
Buccochromis
Caprichromis
Champsochromis
Cheilochromis
Chilotilapia
Copadichromis
Corematodus
Ctenopharynx
Cyrtocara
Dimidiochromis
Diplotaxodon
Docimodus
Eclectochromis
Exochochromis

Fossorochromis
Hemitaeniochromis
Hemitilapia
Lethrinops
Lichnochromis
Mylochromis
Naevochromis
Nimbochromis
Nyassochromis
Otopharynx
Pallidochromis
Placidochromis
Platygnathochromis
Protomelas
Rhamphochromis
Sciaenochromis
Stigmatochromis
Taeniochromis
Taeniolethrinops
Trematocranus
Tramitichromis
Tyrannochromis

C. Mbuna Group
Cyathochromis
Cynotilapia
Genyochromis
Gephyrochromis
Iodotropheus
Labeotropheus
Labidochromis
Melanochromis
Metriaclima
Petrotilapia
Pseudotropheus
Tropheops

II. The Tilapiines
A. Mouthbrooders
Nyasalapia
Oreochromis

B. Substrate Spawners
Tilapia

The two categories of Lake Malawi cichlids can be broken down as follows at the genus level.

General Information about Cichlids

Type of Water and Habitat

The cichlids of Lake Malawi inhabit every conceivable biotope in the lake where oxygen is present. Being a tropical lake, the water is permanently stratified, and there are three distinct layers of water. The first layer is from the surface down to about 250 feet (75 m), the second layer is from 250 (75 m) feet to about 820 feet (250 m), and the last layer is from 820 feet (250 m) to the bottom of the lake. It is only in the upper two layers that oxygen occurs. Winds blowing from a south to north direction along the length of the lake cause the water in the first or upper layer to move or bunch up in the northern part of the lake. This wind effect on the water causes the upper water layer in the north to move downward to the middle layer.

Cichlids reach their zenith in terms of sheer numbers and diversity in Lake Malawi. Pictured is a male Otopharynx lithobates *from Zimbawe Rock.*

In the southern part of the lake, this middle layer rises up, coming up into the upper layer, bringing nutrient-rich waters into the more shallow southern part of the lake. As a result of the nutrient-rich water upwelling in the south, thereby providing more food along the food chain, there are a greater number of cichlid species in this part of the lake.

The lake's cichlids have utilized every possible habitat such as living in the rocks, over the rocks, over the sandy areas of the lake, in grass beds, and even in the deep waters of the lake. Some are almost exclusively found right at the limits of the oxygenated layer of water at a depth of around 820 feet (250 m). Two species even live inside empty snail shells!

The Haplochromines are by far the most important group of cichlids in the lake. Every species in this group practices mouthbrooding for reproductive purposes. All cichlids are egg layers and can be placed into two general categories based on their methods of reproduction: One group lays their eggs on some type of surface, while the other group broods their eggs in their mouth, a process usually performed by the female. Most mouthbrooding species will spawn on some type of surface, such as on top of a rock or on the sand, while there are some that spawn in midwater away from any kind of substrate. Postembryo parental care varies somewhat between species. Some abandon their offspring days after they become fully formed; others care for their young for several months and abandon them when they have

reached a length of nearly 2 inches (5 cm). As a rule, females brood the eggs to full term; however, it has recently been discovered that a male of an undescribed giant *Rhamphochromis* species was captured from deep water holding a mouth full of eggs!

The Tilapiines, although not significant in terms of numbers of species, are nonetheless important from a fisheries perspective. The three endemic *Nyasalapia* species, all of which are mouthbrooders, are important food fish. The single *Oreochromis* species (*O. shiranus*) not endemic to the lake, is also a mouthbrooder. *Tilapia rendalli* is also not endemic and is found over much of central and southern Africa. It is the only cichlid species found in the lake that is a substrate spawner.

Food Items

The cichlids of Lake Malawi have been designed to utilize a wide variety of food items such as aquatic insects and their larvae, mollusks, cichlid eggs and embryos, catfish eggs, zooplankton, phytoplankton, other fish, plants, algae, parasites, fins and scales of cichlids, and

catfish, *Bagrus meridionalis*. This large catfish ignores the presence of the cichlid, and the cichlid is allowed to pick the parasites off the adult catfish. The cichlid also takes advantage of this unique relationship by consuming the catfish's eggs.

Species Flock in Deep Water

One of the more interesting revelations of Lake Malawi's cichlids is the presence of a huge species flock found at depths too deep for scuba diving. Hundreds of species are found in the deeper reaches of the lake at depths of 330 to 820 feet (100–250 m), most being undescribed by science. One undescribed species, *Diplotaxodon sp.* Big Eye, lives at the absolute limits of oxygen penetration at a depth of 820 feet (250 m) and feeds on the aquatic larvae of the lakefly, *Chaoborus edulis*. This species of *Diplotaxodon*, and perhaps other very similar-looking species from this genus, comprise the largest biomass of cichlids found in the lake. One species, *Diplotaxodon limnothrissa*, has an estimated total adult biomass of 87,000 tons, or approximately 1.45 billion adults, not counting juveniles! On full moon nights, a large percentage of *Diplotaxodon sp.* Big Eye ascends to within 10 feet

even the fins and skin of catfishes. The manner that many of these cichlids acquire their specialized food items is fascinating. Some feign death and lay half buried in the sand to attract unsuspecting fishes. Others ram the mouths of brooding females, forcing out the eggs or developing embryos upon which they feed. Some even pick the parasites off other cichlids, much like the famed cleaner wrasses of the tropical Indo-Pacific. Others mimic their prey in body shape and color in order to attack at close range without being noticed. Some may tilt their bodies to focus one eye on their intended prey before lunging forward. One species even feeds on the parasites of a large

Diplotaxodon ecclesi is typical of many deep water cichlids found in the lake, with a silvery background color and whitish and blackish markings on the fins.

(3 m) of the water surface, presumably to feed on migrating lakefly larvae. This is remarkable in light of the fact that cichlids have a closed air bladder, and cannot, presumably, adjust their air bladder as they rise up in the water column—yet this species does! This, and the fact that the species of the genus *Diplotaxodon* have never been seen alive in their natural habitat, even though they represent the largest biomass of cichlids found in the lake, is an indication of how little is understood about the cichlids of Lake Malawi.

The History of Lake Malawi

Lake Malawi came about when the earth's crust ripped apart in the east African continent, creating a long north-to-south tear in the earth's surface. Present-day evidence of this geologic event can be seen in eastern and western shorelines that bear the same overall contours. Rivers that once flowed across the chasm began to pour into the rift and they eventually

Nimbochromis livingstonii feigns death by laying half buried in the sand in order to attract unsuspecting juvenile cichlids. If a juvenile cichlid approaches too closely to the anterior part of the "dead fish," the N. livingstonii will quickly lunge and consume the unsuspecting prey.

Aristochromis christyi often tilts its body at a 45-degree angle along the horizontal axis in order to aim better with one eye before lunging after small fish.

created the lake. The tear in the earth's crust seems to have taken place in the northern four fifths of the lake, since the southern one fifth is significantly shallower and shows no evidence of a tear in the crustal geology. In fact, the area of the lake south of the bottleneck—the narrowest width of the lake, the area between Masinje and Senga Bay—has a wide, flat, or gently sloping lake bottom without any deep underwater ravines like most of the lake. After the ancient Lake Malawi formed, its southern shoreline ended just north of the bottleneck. Eventually, as the water level rose, the southeast and southwest arms of today's lake became the final region of Lake Malawi to be submerged. It is interesting to note that along the coastline, the rocks only penetrate to a depth of around 120 feet (36 m) and then give way to a mixture of mud and sand that slopes down into the abyss. Rocky environs, however, reach down to deeper levels at some isolated islands.

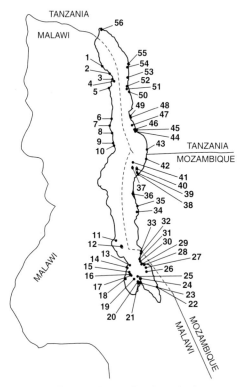

Lake Malawi is 360 miles (600 km) long, and varies between 20 and 45 miles wide. Listed are the various locations around the lake where many Malawi cichlids are collected for the aquarium trade.

1. Ngara
2. Chewere
3. Chilumba
4. Katale Island
5. Chitimba Bay
6. Ruarwe
7. Usisya
8. Lion's Cove
9. Nkhata Bay
10. Mundola
11. Nkhomo Reef
12. Mbenji Island
13. Namalenje Island
14. Senga Bay
15. Nankomo Island
16. Maleri Island
17. Nakantenga Island
18. Chidunga Rocks
19. Mumbo Island
20. Thumbi West Island
21. Otter Island
22. Kadango
23. Cape Maclear
24. Domwe Island
25. Zimbawe Rock
26. Chinyamwezi Island
27. Chinyankwazi Island
28. Eccles Reef
29. West Reef
30. Makanjila Point
31. Fort Maguire
32. Masinje
33. Gome
34. Minos Reef
35. Metangula
36. Tumbi Point
37. Chizumulu Island
38. Cobue
39. Masimbwe Island
40. Likoma Island
41. Taiwan Reef
42. Londo
43. Undu Point
44. Mbamba Bay Island
45. Mbamba Bay
46. Higga Reef
47. Lundo Island
48. Liuli
49. Puulu
50. Lundu
51. Pombo Rocks
52. Ndumbi Point
53. Magunga
54. Cape Kaiser
55. Lupingu
56. Ikombe

11

External anatomy of a cichlid.

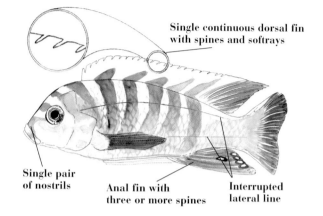

Single continuous dorsal fin
with spines and softrays

Single pair
of nostrils

Anal fin with
three or more spines

Interrupted
lateral line

In the past 140 years, records have been kept indicating that the level of the lake has fluctuated repeatedly, sometimes as much as 25 feet (8 m) in either direction. The level of the lake waters was at its highest in 1980, and since then the level of the lake has receded several yards.

The question of how so many species came to inhabit Lake Malawi is not an easy one to answer. Only a partial explanation can be given for the mbunas that are strictly rock-bound. It has been theorized that as various ancient cichlids invaded the newly formed lake from the surrounding rivers, they began to diversify and evolve into new species. As the level of the lake rose, additional areas of dry land became submerged, which added additional biotopes for the cichlids to colonize. During these processes, various rockbound species became segregated when, in the course of the effects of currents and wave action, rocky areas broke up into isolated stretches separated from one another by substantial sandy zones. These separated populations of species continued to evolve into distinct color variants and new species. However, it is impossible to see how this scenario could have played itself out with the open water species of the Haplochromis group whose present-day numbers are greater than the rockbound mbunas simply because they are not bound to isolated rocky regions, which has presumably been a crucial factor contributing to the evolution of the mbunas.

No plausible answer exists to explain how such a remarkable number of species from the Haplochromis group evolved into the vast numbers that exist today.

This color variant of Cynotilapia afra *hails from Mbenji Island and is known as the Yellow Dorsal Afra.*

General Facts about Lake Malawi

The lake, located in east Africa, is bordered by three countries: Tanzania in the northeast and Mozambique on the central eastern side; the remainder lies within the country of Malawi. It is around 360 miles (580 km) long and varies from 20 to 45 miles (33–73 km) wide with a total shoreline length of approximately 900 miles (1,500 km). It has a maximum depth of 2,300 feet (700 m). This depth is found only on the west side of the lake next to the towns of Ruarwe and Usisya. Oxygen penetrates to a depth of around 820 feet (1,320 km), while below that the water is anoxic, or completely devoid of oxygen. The pH of the water is moderately alkaline, ranging from 7.8 to 8.5, with a carbonate hardness of around 200 to 250 ppm. The temperature of the lake is more or less uniform, regardless of the depth; however, the water temperature varies somewhat depending on the time of year. During the dry season, from June to August, a southeasterly wind called the *mwera* creates an upwelling of the lake's deeper oxygenated and cooler layers, thereby lowering the surface temperatures to around 70°F (21°C) in the southern part of the lake. During the rainy season, from November to April, the average surface temperature ranges from 74° to 80°F (23–27°C). One last aspect of the lake's physical nature is the transparency of the water. Visibility can be as high as 60 feet (18 m) in some places, especially around rocky shorelines or islands where there is a lack of sediments from nearby rivers to cloud the water.

Aulonocara hansbaenschi is closely related to A. stuartgranti. Pictured is a male from Metangula, Mozambique.

What are Cichlids?

Cichlids are members of the order *Perciformes* that possess two fused lower pharyngeal bones (bones located in the throat) in the shape of a triangle, which at a casual glance, appear to be a single bone. The teeth on this fused bone are a good indication of what the particular fish feeds on. For example, if the teeth on the pharyngeal bone are thick with flat tops, the fish is likely to consume hard-shelled organisms such as crustaceans or mollusks. If the teeth are very thin and elongate, the cichlid is likely to consume small soft-bodied organisms such as aquatic insect larvae or plankton. Although well known for this anatomical arrangement, it is not unique to the family *Cichlidae*. This feature is shared by wrasses of the family *Labridae*, the surfperches of the family *Embiotocidae*, and the damselfishes of the family *Pomacentridae*. Additional features that distinguish cichlids are:
✔ a single pair of nostrils
✔ a toothless palate

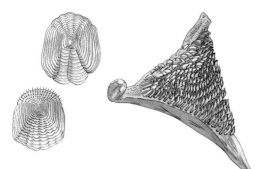

Left: Cycloid (top) and ctenoid scales.
Right: Pharyngeal bone of a typical cichlid.

✔ an interrupted lateral line
✔ an anal fin with three or more spines
✔ scales ctenoid or cycloid
✔ a single continuous dorsal fin composed of spines and soft rays.

Cichlids are also categorized as secondary division freshwater fishes. This means that the ancestor of today's cichlids were marine fishes. At some time in the past, this ancestor invaded and successfully adapted to a freshwater environment.

Additional anatomical structures that set cichlids apart from other kinds of fishes are:
✔ subdivided cheek muscles allowing exact jaw movements
✔ a line showing the fusion point of the two halves of the lower pharyngeal bone
✔ a long deep furrow on the lateral face of the earbones

✔ the opening of the intestine always lying on the left side of the stomach
✔ the first coil of the intestine always lying on the left side of the body.

Cichlids are found throughout many non-tropical to tropical areas of the world. In the Western Hemisphere, they range from southern Texas southward through Central and South America to the northern regions of Argentina and southern Uruguay. They are also present on the Caribbean islands of Cuba and Hispanola. In the Old World, cichlids are found throughout sub-Saharan Africa, Israel, Syria, southern Iran at the Straits of Hormuz, Madagascar, southern India, and Sri Lanka. There are approximately 2,000 species, described and undescribed, with many more likely to be found in the near future. In fact, each year about 20 new species are formally described by ichthyologists.

Lake Malawi

Worldwide distribution of the family Cichlidae.

SETTING UP YOUR AQUARIUM

Aquarium Size and Shape

The habitat preference of Lake Malawi cichlids is either rock-oriented, sand-oriented, or midwater-oriented, or a combination of two or all of these habitats. The size and shape of the aquarium will be determined by the species you intend to maintain.

Lake Malawi cichlids are, by and large, naturally aggressive fishes. When aggressive species are placed in the restricted confines of an aquarium, you are likely to see an increase in aggressive behavior, particularly if the aquarium is too small.

If you decide to maintain rock- or sand-oriented species, you should plan an aquarium with a large amount of bottom space and not as much height. Such an aquarium provides more opportunity to adequately decorate the bottom of the aquarium with rocks and/or sand, which helps these species feel secure. On the other hand, if you decide to maintain midwater-oriented species, an aquarium that is more tall than wide is better, since many mid-

Top: The Aurora, Metriaclima aurora, *is one of the more well-established Mbuna species.*

Bottom: Aulonocara jacobfreibergi *occurs in a variety of geographic color variants around much of the lake. Pictured is a male from Cape Kaiser, in the Tanzanian waters of the lake.*

water-oriented species spend most of their time in the open water column.

It is difficult to give precise instructions on the size aquarium you should have for your Malawian cichlids, but a few guidelines can be suggested. The cichlids of Lake Malawi come in a wide range of sizes, from tiny *Labidochromis* and some *Pseudotropheus* species, which attain a length of 2½ inches (6 cm), to the large, predatory species of the genus *Tyrannochromis, Champsochromis, Nimbochromis,* and *Buccochromis,* all of which can reach lengths of 12 inches (30 cm) and more. If you plan on maintaining the smaller mbuna species, a small aquarium of approximately 20 to 30 gallons (76–114 L) will suffice. For a great majority of Lake Malawi cichlids, whose average size is approximately 4 to 7 inches (10–18 cm), a larger aquarium of approximately 50 to 100 gallons (189–379 L) is necessary. Going to the other extreme, if you choose to maintain the largest species, such as any *Tyrannochromis, Champsochromis,* or *Buccochromis* species, an aquarium of at least 250 gallons (946 L) is strongly recommend. Approximately ½ inch (12 mm) of fish length per gallon (4 L) of aquarium water is a good rule of thumb to follow. Be careful in calculating this, however, since nearly all aquariums sold do not hold the exact number of gallons specified on the label. In order to properly calculate the volume of water in your aquarium, measure on the inside of the aquarium in inches and multiply the length by the height by the width, and then divide by 231.

Another factor that will determine the size of your aquarium is the number of fish you plan to maintain. Think ahead and decide which species and how many of each you plan to maintain, then get the appropriate aquarium size and shape.

The Aquarium Stand

Aquariums are heavy for their size, and a sturdy, stable stand must be provided. Water weighs approximately 8 pounds per gallon (4 kg per 4 L), and added to the total weight of the water is the weight of the aquarium and the decorations in it. Not only does the stand need to be sturdy enough to handle all the weight, it also needs to be level, so that no one area of the aquarium or stand receives more weight and pressure than necessary. If a stand

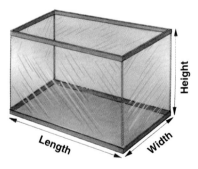

Mathematical equation for calculating the number of gallons of your aquarium: Measuring on the inside of the aquarium in inches, multiply the width by the height by the length and then divide by 231.

or aquarium is not completely horizontal, placing a penny or two under the uneven portion of the stand or aquarium works well.

Types of Filtration

Filtration is the most important aspect of proper aquarium fish husbandry and needs to be understood before you can successfully maintain any fish in the restrictions of a captive environment. In order to safely maintain fishes in an aquarium, their water must be filtered (processed). There are three types of aquarium filtration and a combination of all three is ideal.

Biological Filtration

The first and most important type of filtration is biological. Any organic material, such as fish waste, uneaten food, decaying plant matter, or dead rotting fish, is mineralized by heterotrophic bacteria, resulting in the production of ammonia, which is exceedingly toxic to fishes. Additional bacteria further oxidize the ammonia into nitrite, and still other bacteria convert the nitrite to nitrate. This is the nitrification process, or biological filtration in its simplest form.

When you first install a biological filter, it takes approximately four to six weeks to grow enough bacteria to efficiently process your fishes' excrement, uneaten food, and decaying plant matter. A common method employed to begin the four- to six-week maturation process is to use "test fishes." These can be any species of tropical fishes that is extremely hardy and can withstand high concentrations of ammonia and nitrites. Some of the more commonly used test fishes are the Paradise Gourami (*Macropodus*

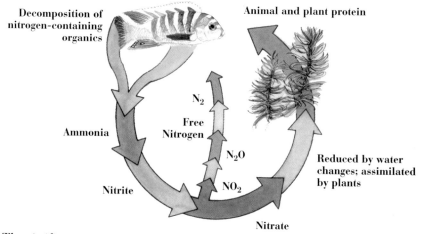

Decomposition of
nitrogen-containing
organics

Animal and plant protein

N_2

Free
Nitrogen

Ammonia

N_2O

NO_2

Reduced by water
changes; assimilated
by plants

Nitrite

Nitrate

The nitrification process in an aquarium.

opercularis) and the Blue Gourami (*Trichogaster trichopterus*). These labyrinth fishes will normally survive the spike of ammonia and nitrite during the cycling process. Test fishes should be maintained and fed daily in the newly set up aquarium until it has cycled. It is advisable not to perform any water changes during this period. After the aquarium has cycled, perform a 50 percent water change, remove the test fishes, and add your prized Malawian cichlids.

A suitable way to follow the cycling process of your biological filter is to invest in test kits

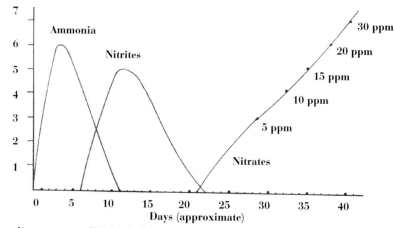

The cycling process of biological filtration.

for ammonia, nitrite, and nitrate. Test your newly set up aquarium daily and monitor any change that takes place, or you can have your water tested at any reputable tropical fish dealer. Over the course of the first few days, you will see a spike in the amount of ammonia in the water. As the ammonia recedes to negligible levels, the nitrites will spike, then the nitrites will slowly recede to negligible levels as you begin to get your first nitrate readings. When nitrites are no longer present, the aquarium has matured and the cycle is complete.

Biological filtration also produces hydrogen ions that lower the pH, making the water more acidic. The easiest way to combat this is to maintain a regular schedule of water changes. Frequent water changes will help to maintain a stable environment for your Malawian cichlids. In addition to preventing the water from becoming acidic, water changes will help to lower the nitrate levels. The overall well-being of your aquarium residents depends on regularly changing the water.

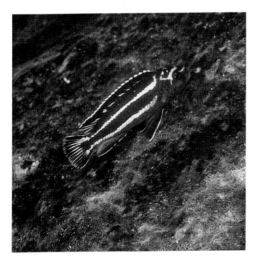

Chemical Filtration

The second form of filtration is chemical, which may consist of carbon or various pelleted resins used to absorb harmful chemicals from the water. This type of filtration is useful if you live in an area where your local municipal water supply is contaminated with a variety of chemicals. Chemical filtration is also useful for removing medications from the water after medicines have effected a cure.

Mechanical Filtration

The third form of filtration is mechanical. This form of filtration simply removes visible particulate matter as water passes through a filtering medium so that the water remains free of unsightly sediments.

Whatever form of filtration you decide to use, it should biologically filter the water in a consistent and adequate manner. It should also mechanically filter the water to remove visible organic material, and it should have the capacity to chemically filter the water to remove any harmful chemicals that may be present. You will need to make sure that the filter does not become clogged with organic material, thereby producing excessive amounts of nitrates. Regularly servicing your filter and performing water changes on a regular basis will help to keep the nitrates low, as well as prevent the water from becoming acidic.

The habitat of the Lake Malawi cichlids you intend to maintain should be reproduced as closely as possible. Pictured is a male **Melanchromis johanni** *from Masinje, swimming over a large rock.*

Aquarium Water Chemistry

Since the cichlids of Lake Malawi are from water that has a moderately high pH and alkalinity, it would be wise to attempt to match your aquarium water to that of the lake. It may be impossible to precisely duplicate the water chemistry of Lake Malawi in your aquarium, but you can condition your aquarium water in the right direction, and in doing so, achieve a modest facsimile. The pH in the lake ranges from about 7.8 to 8.5 with a total mineral hardness of 200 to 220 ppm of carbonate hardness (or 12 to 13 kH of German hardness), making the water rather alkaline with a moderately high mineral concentration. Most municipal water comes out of the faucet with a pH of approximately 7.2 to 7.6 and a total mineral hardness that may vary substantially depending on your local water source. If your water comes close to the pH and hardness range of water in Lake Malawi, the water can be used straight from the faucet. It is recommended that you invest in test kits that measure for pH and water hardness, or at least have your water tested at a local retail tropical fish store so that you will be able to determine whether your water needs buffering to increase the pH and kH. If your aquarium needs to be buffered to increase the pH and kH, there are a number of products on the market that you can use.

The important thing to remember is that you should maintain consistency when using these products. Each time water changing is needed, additional lake salts to buffer the water back up should be mixed in with the new water

Metriaclima zebra received its species name due to the male's breeding dress, as seen in this dominant male from Likoma Island.

before it is added back into the aquarium. If you choose to have gravel in the aquarium, a thin layer of crushed coral sand or oyster shells will probably be the substrate of choice, since either material will continually leach out enough minerals to keep the water on the alkaline side. If your tap water is already alkaline and hard, an inert gravel such as silica sand may be used instead.

If you live in an area where your tap water has a relatively high pH and kH, all you need to do is add a water conditioner to remove any chlorine, chloramine, heavy metals, or other contaminants. Remember to add water conditioner to all new water that you put into your aquarium.

Heater and Thermometer

Malawian cichlids come from water with a temperature that ranges from 70° to 80°F (25.5°–28°C); therefore, a heater is usually necessary. Aquariums up to 100 gallons (378.5 L) will probably need only one appropriately sized heater, while aquariums much larger should have two heaters—one at each end of

*This **Auloncara jacobfreibergi** from Otter Island was one of the first variants collected for the hobby.*

*This variant of **Cynotilapia afra** from Lupingu, Tanzania shows a darker pattern than is typical of many C. afra.*

the aquarium—for greater temperature stability. You will need to read the suggested heater size on the box of the heater before making a purchase; it will give you a guideline regarding size and wattage needed for your aquarium. A general guide to follow is about 3 watts per gallon; for example, a 50-gallon (189 L) aquarium would need a 150-watt heater. The heater should be mounted in the aquarium only after it is full of water. Remember to allow about half an hour for the heater's internal thermostat to adjust itself to the temperature of the water before turning on your heater. At this point, install an accurate thermometer.

Lighting

Proper lighting enables you to observe your Malawian cichlids more clearly. The main lighting of choice is a fluorescent bulb. However, many Malawian cichlids live deep enough in their natural habitat that the amount of light that penetrates their domain is substantially reduced. It is therefore recommended that you use only one bulb, since too much lighting will wash out the colors of your Malawi cichlids, and they will not look their best. A blue actinic bulb will help to bring out the natural blue colors of many Malawi cichlids. Also, cichlids need to sleep as much as we do, so keep the lights on only during the day, and turn them off at night.

Decorations

Determining what kind of decorations to use will depend on what species of Malawian cichlid you plan to keep. As previously mentioned, Malawi cichlids have three general habitat preferences: rock-oriented, sand-oriented, and midwater-oriented. If you plan on maintaining rock-oriented species, several rocks should be piled up to form caves and passageways for them to find refuge in and to establish territories. Rocks should be relatively smooth. Jagged lava rocks should be avoided since they may injure your Malawian cichlids if they acciden-

The Red Empress, Protomelas cf. taeniola-*tus, from Namalenje Island is one of the most popular "Haps." Today, most Red Empress offered for sale are from captive-raised stock.*

tally scrape against the sharp edges. Use only enough sand to cover the bottom of the aquarium. Rock-oriented Malawi cichlids are prodigious diggers, and will pile up sand/gravel into unsightly heaps. If very large rocks are used, a small piece of Styrofoam can be placed underneath the sections of the rock that will be in contact with the glass. This will protect the bottom pane.

For the sand-oriented species, a shallow layer of fine silica sand is preferred. Only a few smooth rocks should be present, strategically placed so as to serve as territorial boundaries. These few rocks may also provide a degree of refuge from other fishes and a greater sense of security in the restrictions of an aquarium.

For the midwater-oriented species, a shallow layer of silica sand and a couple of smooth stones will suffice, since they will be spending most of their time in the upper water column.

The background can be decorated with dark blue or black background sheets from your local tropical fish dealer. Prefabricated rock molds designed to be glued onto the inside back of the aquarium provide a realistic deco-ration for a Malawian cichlid aquarium.

Sand/Gravel

Most of us want to have some sand or gravel in our aquariums. Not only is it pleasing to the eye, it hides the bottom of the aquarium from view; however, having too much sand or gravel will invite bacteria to form anaerobic

conditions in the deeper recesses of the gravel bed. If you maintain an undergravel filter, a standard 2 inches (5 cm) of gravel depth will suffice. Barring this type of filtration, a fine layer of no more than ½ inch (1.3 cm) of sand or gravel will be enough. If you plan to maintain sand-oriented Malawian cichlids, silica sand is ideal.

Live Plants

The only place in Lake Malawi where plants are found are near river mouths and shallow bays along the shoreline and at some islands. They provide protection for juvenile sand-oriented cichlids, and at least one species of cichlid feeds on them. They are not particularly attractive plants, and do not figure into the biotopes of most of the Malawi cichlids main-tained in captivity. It is therefore not recom-mended that they be maintained with Malawi cichlids. Their strong lighting requirements will wash out the colors of your Malawi cichlids, and if you maintain rock-oriented species, they will uproot the plants by their instinctive dig-ging behavior.

There are many types of filters on the market. Most do a fair job of maintaining adequate water quality, but some are more efficient than others. Learn about the most popular types before you decide on the best one for your cichlids.

Undergravel Filter

Undergravel filters have long been popular for both salt- and freshwater aquariums. A plate is placed under the gravel; water is drawn down through the gravel by a submersible water pump or air-driven stone, through the plate, and circulated back into the aquarium via a tube at the back end of the plate. Bacteria accumulate in the gravel bed so that the gravel bed becomes one big biological filter. These filters provide satisfactory biological filtration initially, but eventually they become saturated with organic material and become nitrate-producing factories. They per-

form an average job at providing mechanical filtration but provide absolutely no chemical filtration. Organic material eventually translates into the production of nitrates through the nitrification process, so it is important to remove as much organic material as possible to keep nitrates at a minimum. This is nearly impossible with undergravel filters. Over time, this type of filter collects more organic material than you will be able to remove, particularly below the plates, resulting in the production of high levels of nitrates, regardless of frequent large-scale water changes and gravel vacuuming.

Trickle Filter

The trickle filter is an excellent biological filter, particularly if you wish to filter large aquariums. Oxygen saturation is achieved in this filter as the drops of water trickle through the ball-like filter medium. The

pre-filter serves as the mechanical portion of this filter and there is a small chamber next to the filter medium in which to place chemical filtering material. Over time, the plastic balls and other internal parts of the filter gather more and more organic material, which, in turn, produces large quantities of nitrates. If the plastic balls are occasionally flushed of their organic buildup, and/or a small portion is periodically replaced with new plastic balls, excessive amounts of nitrates should not be a problem. Also, as part of regularly maintaining any filter, you will need to examine the inside of the filter to make sure it is functioning optimally and remove any buildup of organic material from the walls and floor of the filter, as well as from the intake and outtake tubes.

Canister Filter

Canister filters provide the three types of filtration already mentioned; however, they require a lot of servicing to keep the collection of organic material inside the canister to a minimum. They can be difficult and messy to clean, something that most of us use as an excuse to put off regular maintenance. It is important to keep the pre-

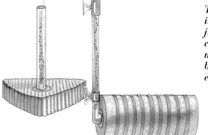

The sponge filter is ideal for raising juvenile Malawi cichlids. The spongy medium prevents babies from being entrapped.

FILTERS

filter clean so that water flow through the canister is not impeded.

Box Filter

Box filters are capable of providing all three types of biological filtration, but must be serviced frequently in order to keep organic material from building up to the point of producing large amounts of nitrates. Some hobbyists have modified box filters to contain only dime-sized lava rocks in the lower half of the chamber, while having a thick piece of sponge on the top half of the chamber. The lava rock provides the surface space for nitrifying bacteria to colonize, and thus provides for biological filtration, while the sponge serves primarily as a pre-filter, reducing organic material buildup on the lava rocks. This type of filter seems to work best when the sponge is rinsed thoroughly once a week. It is ideal for aquariums no larger than 30 or 40 gallons (113.5 or 151 L).

Sponge Filter

Sponge filters are excellent for small aquariums and for raising juvenile fishes; their surface area is too small to entrap juvenile fishes. Eventually, the sponge will break down and need to be replaced, so the process of reestablishing a biologically mature filter must be repeated. You can avoid this by starting up another sponge filter two months before replacing the old one.

Fluidized Bed Filter

Another filter on the market is the fluidized bed filter. This type is a more efficient biological filter than those previously mentioned. Unless a pre-filter is attached to the intake valve of the fluidized bed filter, it will provide no mechanical filtration and the fine sand in

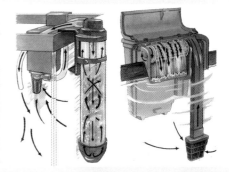

The fluidized bed filter (left) is one of the newest filters on the market; it provides excellent biological filtration. The biological wheel filter (right) is another excellent aquarium filter; it provides all three types of filtration in an efficient arrangement.

this filter will eventually clog, reducing its efficiency. It also does not provide any chemical filtration.

Biological Wheel Filter

The biological wheel filter provides all three types of filtration. This type of filter can be quickly and easily cleaned of its organic buildup without compromising its biological filtering capabilities. This filter has a corrugated wheel in the pathway of the water return. As water is returned to the aquarium, it pours over the corrugated wheel, which, once mature, contains the bacteria necessary for biological filtration. This arrangement also enables oxygen to saturate the water, something needed not only by fish, but also by the nitrifying bacteria. The back chamber of this filter provides for mechanical and chemical filtration in the form of a filter pad that can easily be replaced before clogging with organic material.

MAINTAINING THE AQUARIUM

Water Changes

Changing water on a regular basis is the single most important task of aquarium fish keeping. Several factors will determine when, how much, and how often you should change your aquarium water. The number of Malawian cichlids you are maintaining, the amount of food given at each feeding, and how many times a day they are fed will determine your water-changing routines. Approximately 25 percent of the volume of the aquarium's water should be changed weekly, or 33 percent every two weeks in an aquarium that is sparsely populated ($\frac{1}{2}$ inch [12.7 mm] of fish per gallon). If you crowd your Malawian cichlids (1 to 2 inches [2.5–5 cm] of fish per gallon), then 50 percent water changes weekly, or 75 percent water changes every two weeks should be standard procedure. These are rough guidelines to follow, and you may need to change more or less water, depending on the number of fish and the quantity of food given.

It is vitally important to know the husbandry requirements of Lake Malawi cichlids, and then to faithfully implement them in your aquarium. Pictured is a male **Metriaclima mbenjii** *from Mbenji Island.*

Test Kits

Invest in quality test kits. Once your biological filter has cycled, you will primarily be testing for nitrate levels, which will give you an indication when a water change is required. Ideally, your Malawi cichlids should not be exposed to nitrate concentrations beyond 20 ppm for extended lengths of time. Many experts agree that exposure to significant levels of nitrates for extended periods weakens a fish's immune system and suppresses reproduction.

How can you know if your water changing is keeping the nitrates at an acceptably low level? Before each regular water change, test the water for nitrates, and keep a log of the readings for several weeks. If the readings show that the nitrates are slowly increasing in spite of your regular water changing, that will indicate you need to perform larger or more frequent water changes. It may also indicate that you need to take special care to remove as much detritus as possible with each water change. If you have an undergravel filter in place, or have a thin layer of sand or gravel without an undergravel filter, you will need to gravel vacuum the sand or gravel during each water change. If you are using box or power filters, this will probably entail removing the mechanical filtering portion, rinsing off the accumulated detritus, and/or throwing it away and replacing it with a new one. You may also need to reduce the amount of food you offer your Malawi cichlids. The key is to remove as much detritus from the aquarium as quickly as possible.

It is important to acquire healthy Malawi cichlids for your aquarium. Even if the Malawi cichlids you want to purchase look outwardly healthy, such as having no clamped fins and no

Siphoning water from the aquarium is the most efficient way to perform a water change. If the aquarium is large, siphoning the water out—via a garden hose—into the yard is recommended. For small aquariums, siphon the water into a bucket, then dispense with the water elsewhere. Always siphon from the bottom of the aquarium, particularly if you have an undergravel filter and are using a gravel vacuum.

scratching on rocks, the water quality may have elevated levels of nitrates in the dealer's aquariums. It is not uncommon for some retail stores, particularly large supermarket-sized pet stores, to maintain their tropical fishes in water with extremely high nitrates. It might be advisable to ask what the nitrate level is before you purchase your Malawi cichlid. Perhaps the water could be tested before a purchase is made.

Siphoning

A siphon hose is an important item of equipment for performing water changes. Water from the bottom of the aquarium should be siphoned out, and if you have sand or gravel in your aquarium, a modified siphon hose with a wide mouth at the intake end is recommended. This widened end should be placed into the sand or gravel so that the siphoning action will lift the detritus out while leaving the substrate behind.

Any new water being placed back into the aquarium should first be thoroughly conditioned with a name-brand water conditioner. The temperature of the new water should be the same as that of the aquarium water, and never cooler.

Aeration

The aquarium water should be saturated with oxygen at all times. A clear sign that not enough oxygen is available can be ascertained when you see your Malawian cichlids gasping for oxygen near the surface of the aquarium. Making sure that enough oxygen is present in the water can be accomplished by the use of an airstone-driven filter inside the aquarium or an outside power filter that sufficiently agitates the water's surface via the outflow from the filtering chamber.

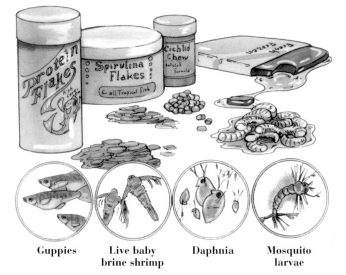

Guppies   Live baby   Daphnia   Mosquito
brine shrimp   larvae

A varied diet is important for the overall well-being of your Malawi cichlids.

Diet

In the wild, Malawi cichlids consume a wide variety of foods. In their natural habitat, Malawian cichlids will consume other kinds of foods for which they were not specifically designed; for example, species of the genus *Petrotilapia*, considered herbivorous, will not hesitate to eat baby fishes if given the opportunity. Therefore, some flexibility in the diet of Malawian cichlids is permissible, but their primary food source should constitute the bulk of their diet. (See dietary requirements for individual species in the chapter beginning on page 40.) It is recommended that you vary their diet, and not overfeed them. Overfed Malawian cichlids will not look their best, may become lethargic, and may cease to show any interest in spawning. They also might grow to hideously large sizes, sizes that they would never reach in the wild. It is always a good idea not to give your cichlids all they can consume in one feeding. If they are kept slightly hungry, they will always be on the prowl for food, and thus spend much of their time actively swimming about in the open.

Parasites and Bacterial Infections

There are a multitude of parasites and bacterial infections sporadically encountered in tropical fishes, but only a few seem to be recurrent problems with Malawi cichlids. The easiest thing you can do to minimize the risk of your cichlids having a particular ailment—parasite or bacterial infection—is to practice good husbandry skills. These skills will assure a healthy environment that will in turn result in healthy, vigorous cichlids. It is only when the needs of your cichlids are not being met that they begin to become stressed. The immune system weakens considerably when they become stressed and they will not be able to

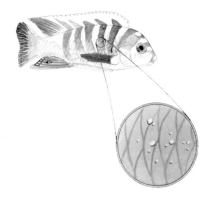

The parasite ich is commonly encountered with Malawi cichlids.

fight off an encroaching parasitic or bacterial infection. The result will often be that your Malawi cichlid develops a debilitating ailment that will need medicinal treatment if it is to survive. If your Malawi cichlid comes down with a parasite or a bacterial infection, the following information may be helpful.

Ichthyophtirius

Ich, or *Ichthyophtirius multifilis*, is probably the most commonly encountered parasite to

The parasite ich is commonly encountered with Malawi cichlids.

attack fishes in the aquarium. It appears when fishes are stressed due to a sudden drop in temperature. This parasite may not manifest itself for several days, and may only attach itself inside the gills of the host fish. If ich confines itself to the gills, it will be nearly impossible to detect at first. When ich attacks in this manner, it may not be uncommon for your fish to die, seemingly for no apparent reason. At other times, you will see tiny white dots sprinkled over the fish's body, something like the color and size of salt grains. In whichever region of the body ich manifests itself, the affected fish will probably be seen to glance off objects in an effort to scratch itself. Fortunately, this is one of the easiest parasitic infections to treat. Malachite green is the most readily available medicine you can use to treat ich. Ich has a three-day life cycle, so the medicine should be present in the water for at least three days, four to five being better. It is important to remove any carbon from your filter before using medicine, since the carbon will absorb the medicine, rendering it ineffective. A slight rise in water temperature will help to speed up the life cycle of the ich and help the medicine effect a cure a little sooner. A 25 to 50 percent water change after the completion of treatment is advisable along with the addition of fresh carbon to absorb any residual medication that may still be present in your aquarium.

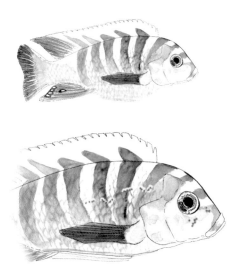

Good husbandry practices help prevent bloat (top) and hole-in-the-head disease (bottom).

Bloat

Another ailment that commonly effects Malawi cichlids, particularly those species that tend to be herbivorous, is bloat. Bloat is caused when the intestinal tract of the fish becomes infected/inflamed. The inflammation is usually caused by a combination of improper diet; for example, feeding herbivorous species a disproportionate amount of high-protein foods, or too much of the same kind of food, followed by poor water quality. This condition, unless treated immediately, may result in the death of the fish within a few days. If treated immediately upon signs of first symptoms (loss of appetite, a noticeable distention of the body region, and an increased respiratory rate), a cure may be possible, but is not always guaranteed. Use the medication metronidazole at $\frac{1}{8}$ teaspoon per 10 gallons (38 L) of water once a day for three to five days. After the completion of treatment, perform a 50 percent water change and add carbon to the filter to absorb any residual medication. Again, prevention is the best strategy: Feed the proper foods, taking particular care not to overfeed, and maintain a clean aquarium.

Hole-in-the-Head

Hole-in-the-head, or lateral line disease, is caused by an infestation of flagellate protozoans attacking the sensory pores of a fish's head, as well as its lateral line. It is indirectly brought on by poor husbandry practices. Cichlids with this infection show pitting on the sides of the face and on the lateral line system on the body. Some species seem to be more

Since Lake Malawi cichlids are aggressive fishes, no new individuals should be added to a well-stocked aquarium. Consider setting up another aquarium to house any new acquisitions. Pictured are two dominant male **Pseudotropheus** *sp. Masimbwe Elongatus fighting over coveted territory.*

Even though quite rare in the wild,
Nimbochromis venustus *is quite common
in captivity due to commercial breeding.*

prone to developing this malady than others, and you can keep its occurrence down to a minimum by maintaining scrupulous aquarium conditions and making sure that your cichlids are being fed a well-balanced diet. Metronidazole may stop it from spreading, but once the damage has been done, the pitting on the face and lateral line of the cichlid will always be present in the form of a scar. Often, nothing will stop the spread of the disease and the only thing that can be done is to euthanize the infected fish.

Quarantine and the Hospital Aquarium

A method often employed by hobbyists and professionals alike is the use of a quarantine aquarium to house newly acquired fish. Malawi cichlids may be stressed, and may carry a bacterial infection or internal or external parasites in the dealer's holding tank. If they were to be placed directly into your main aquarium with your other fishes, the newly introduced Malawi cichlid might infect the other aquarium inhabitants. This can be a very frustrating experience and is one that we have all gone through as novice aquarists. A quarantine aquarium need only be a 10-gallon (9.5 L) aquarium. It should have a biological filter up and running, such as an outside power filter or inside sponge filter, but no chemical filtration. A heater and thermometer is needed to maintain a constant temperature of 80°F (26.7°C). There should be no gravel in the aquarium since it will make it more difficult to keep the aquarium clean during treatment. The aquarium should not be lit overhead, and enough shelter should be placed into the aquarium so that the quarantined fish will feel safe and secure. If the fish is stressed because it cannot find a place to hide, it may not respond as quickly to treatment.

With a quarantine aquarium set up and running properly, any newly acquired fish should be placed into it for approximately one month. During this time, the quarantined fish is cared for in the same manner as you would any other aquarium fish. If the fish does have a bacterial infection or parasites, it will become apparent within a month. At first sign of such ailments, the quarantined fish should be treated with the proper medication until it is completely cured. Only then should it be placed into the main aquarium. Remove any leftover medication that may still be present in the quarantine aquarium with the addition of fresh carbon to the filter.

The quarantine aquarium may also double as a hospital aquarium for Malawi cichlids in your main aquarium that become injured or come down with an infection. This way, instead of treating the main aquarium, the fish in question can be removed and placed in the hospital aquarium for individualized treatment.

This captive raised Firecrest Mloto, Copadichromis virginalis, is best maintained with non-aggressive species, since its mild disposition will not enable it to compete with more aggressive species.

Female Metriaclima estherae from Minos Reef, Mozambique show the most brilliant orange coloration of any variant along the Mozambique coastline.

Adding New Malawi Cichlids to an Established Aquarium

If you are considering adding new Malawi cichlids to your aquarium, make sure there is plenty of room and open areas for the addition of more fishes. This may not always be possible considering the territorial nature of many Malawi cichlids. Often, a newly introduced Malawi cichlid will be bullied, perhaps even killed, because the other inhabitants have already had time to establish themselves and acquire territories. The new fish, without any territory in a new environment, is automatically placed on the bottom of the pecking order. To avoid this, you can rearrange the decorations when you add a new fish, thereby giving all the cichlids an equal chance at procuring and establishing a territory. Or, when you first stock your aquarium, do so all

This color mutation of Metriaclima zebra from Thumbi West Island is devoid of any black pigment, giving it an almost albinolike appearance.

at once so that all the fishes will become equally established. If you want to acquire additional fishes and your aquarium is already firmly established, then consider setting up another aquarium or two.

SPAWNING TIPS FOR LAKE MALAWI CICHLIDS

Setting the Groundwork

One rewarding facet of maintaining Malawian cichlids is inducing them to spawn. The first step is to decide which species of Malawi cichlid you wish to try, taking into consideration your aquarium limitations and available funds, then set out to acquire specimens. A reputable tropical fish dealer or specialty cichlid club are two sources that may offer a wide variety of Malawian cichlids. Some hobbyists choose to start out with wild-caught adults, while others begin with captive-raised juveniles. You need to be careful with the latter method since, in all probability, the juveniles you purchase may have originated from the same parents, and what ends up happening is that brother and sister are bred to each other. The inbred juveniles are then bred back to each other, and so on. Inbreeding for several generations results in a deterioration in quality so that the unfortunate Malawi cichlid loses all of its original appeal and is virtually worthless. For example, *Pseudotropheus saulosi* should have a sky blue body with several dark blue vertical bands through the entire body, but some captive-bred specimens show no dark vertical barring. This is clearly unacceptable, and these poor-quality cichlids should never be permitted to reproduce.

Avoiding Inbreeding

There are two things you can do to minimize this often repeated practice of inbreeding. The first is to work with wild-caught specimens. If you are not able to afford or find wild-caught specimens, the second option is to obtain high-quality captive-bred stock. High-quality captive-bred specimens are those with the color and body shape closely matching that of wild-caught species.

When obtaining captive-bred juveniles, make an effort to buy one or two specimens from different sources so that the likelihood of spawning brother to sister will be greatly diminished. Every effort to propagate wild-caught or high-quality captive-bred stock is crucial.

Habitats for Spawning

For the rock-oriented species, or Mbuna, the landscape of the aquarium should consist of a large number of rocks piled up to form passageways and places of refuge. Territories will be formed in and around the rocks, and spawning will likely occur among the rocks.

When attempting to spawn Lake Malawi cichlids, it is always important to obtain quality specimens. Avoid those specimens with improper coloration or abnormal shapes and sizes. Pictured is a school of juvenile Tyrannochromis macrostoma.

There are hundreds of undescribed species of cichlids in Lake Malawi. Pictured is one from shallow waters off the east coast of the lake near Masinje. It is likely a species of the genus **Protomelas**.

For the sand- and midwater-oriented species, the layout of the aquarium should be as open as possible. Only a thin layer of sand and a couple of smooth stones to demarcate boundaries and provide some security to a brooding female should be included.

Difficult-to-Spawn Species

Some naturally aggressive species may prove challenging to spawn in captivity. Dominant males may kill other males or unreceptive females, or even brooding females if not enough hiding places are provided. In some circumstances, no amount of hiding places will prevent particularly aggressive males from wreaking havoc. This may seem insurmountable if you have your heart set on maintaining and spawning a particularly aggressive species. Fortunately, there are a couple of things you can do to minimize the aggression and encourage peaceful spawning.

1. Crowd your aquarium with the species you wish to work with and remove all possible hiding places. This will have the effect of spreading out the aggression of the dominant male so that he does not focus on any one fish. If he is faced with too many of his own kind to chase after, the dominant male might become more mellow with this arrangement, but close attention must be given to maintaining good water quality. Stocking an aquarium to its limits is risky and will result in greater quantities of waste being produced. The buildup of waste products must be dealt with by significantly increased water changing and frequently examining, cleaning, or replacing the disposable filter pad of your filter to make sure it is functioning capably.

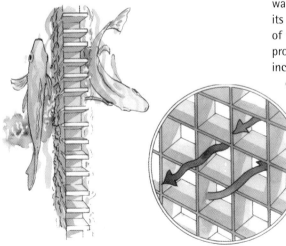

An aquarium divider is a practical way to spawn highly aggressive Malawi cichlids. The holes in the divider permit the male to fertilize the female's eggs, while at the same time preventing the male from overly harassing, or even killing, the female.

This male **Copadichromis borleyi** *from Eccles Reef shows the typical long ventral fins seen in most species of* **Copadichromis.**

The least known color variant of Otopharynx lithobates *is this white-dorsalled male from Thumbi West Island. The orange-dorsalled variant is more commonly referred to as the Red Top Aristochromis.*

Metriaclima estherae *is one of a handful of Mbuna species that produce blotched color mutations.*

A male and female **Protomelas** cf. **taeniolatus** *from Mbenji Island in the act of spawning.*

2. Divide the aquarium in two with a single male on one side and a single female on the other side. An egg crate, a light-diffusing ventilated panel, works well. It can be found in the lighting department of your local hardware store. When the pair is ready to spawn, they will do so next to the divider. The male's sperm will easily pass through the divider and fertilize the female's eggs. The female can then brood her clutch of eggs without being molested.

Raising Juvenile Malawi Cichlids

Baby Brine Shrimp

One of the best foods for juvenile Malawi cichlids is live baby brine shrimp, *Artemia nauplii*. They are easy to hatch and make an excellent first food. Brine shrimp eggs can be obtained through your local tropical fish dealer, or from specialty companies that advertise in aquarium-related magazines. Finely crushed flake food can also be offered in addition to the live baby brine shrimp. After feeding your juvenile Malawi cichlids, any uneaten food or waste on the bottom of the aquarium should be siphoned out on a daily basis. As the fishes grow and consume more food, it will be necessary to get the young fishes accustomed to larger, more frequent water changes of 25 to 50 percent weekly.

In order to set up a continuous supply of live baby brine shrimp:

Steps 1 and 2   Steps 3 and 4

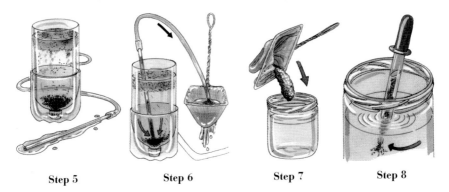

Step 5   Step 6   Step 7   Step 8

Hatching brine shrimp eggs (see illustration and text).

A school of juvenile **Nimbochromis polystigma** *from Thumbi West Island.*

1. Cut four empty 2-liter soda bottles according to illustration.

2. Invert the longer-cut bottles and place them upside down into the shorter-cut bottles. Make sure that the lids on the inverted bottles are firmly in place.

3. Fill both inverted containers with water and add 2 to 3 tablespoons of rock salt to each. Insert the rigid tubing, connected to an air pump with flexible tubing, into each container all the way to the bottom of the inverted container.

4. Add one teaspoon of brine shrimp eggs to one container only.

5. Wait 36 to 48 hours until the water takes on an orange cast. At this point, remove the rigid tubing and allow the eggs and shrimp to settle. The live baby brine shrimp will settle to the bottom of the container.

6. Take another piece of rigid tubing attached to flexible tubing. With the rigid end, siphon the live baby brine shrimp from the bottom of the container into a baby brine shrimp net.

7. Pour the live baby brine shrimp from the baby brine shrimp net into a small container of water.

8. Using an eyedropper, dispense the live baby brine shrimp from the small container.

One day after the first container of brine shrimp eggs hatch, begin the second container following steps 4 through 8. One day after this second container hatches, rinse out the first container and start a new batch as you begin to dispense the live baby brine shrimp from the second container. Repeating this procedure will give you a constant supply of live baby brine shrimp for your juvenile Malawi cichlids.

The most rewarding way to obtain offspring from parental Malawi cichlids is to let them do what comes naturally. One of the most satisfying experiences you'll have in spawning Malawi cichlids will be to observe and study the behavior of the parents and juveniles. There may come a time when you want to separate the babies from a brooding female or from the main breeding aquarium and raise them on their own, particularly when the numbers of juveniles begin to crowd the aquarium.

Removing Juveniles to a Separate Aquarium

If you opt to let the brooding female hold to full term in a community aquarium, the juveniles will eventually be released to find refuge among the rocks. At this point, the only practical way to remove them from the aquarium is to remove all the rocks, and carefully net them out, one by one. If you have a large, sparsely populated aquarium, consider letting the juveniles grow up alongside the adults. Many will be consumed along the way, but a few will make it to adulthood.

Most hobbyists choose to strip a brooding female or remove it to another aquarium. Try removing the brooding female while she is asleep. Gently prod the female into a shallow container or jar. Once in the container, remove the container with the female into another previously set up aquarium (preferably 10 gallons [38 L]) where the female can brood her young to full term and release them unmolested. This separate aquarium should be furnished with ample hiding places so that the brooding female will feel secure.

Removing Eggs or Juveniles from a Brooding Female

Evidence that a spawning has taken place will be apparent when you see one or more females with a bulge in their throats, indicating that they are incubating a clutch of eggs. To save most of the spawn, many hobbyists choose to strip the female of her eggs and hatch them artificially. The most trouble-free way to catch the female is while she is asleep. Wait until the lights have been out for several hours, then turn on the lights and immediately catch the female with a net before she wakes up. This way, the female will not panic. Gently grab her with a wet hand, and with a sharpened pencil in the other hand, carefully pry open her mouth, gently shaking her in and out of the water while holding her over the net. The developing embryos or juveniles should begin to trickle out into the net. Continue this process until they have all been expelled from the female's mouth. Afterwards, return the female to the spawning aquarium or, if needed, place her in another aquarium to recuperate. If fully formed juveniles are released, quickly place them into the grow-out aquarium that you've prepared beforehand with water from the parents' aquarium. If embryos are released, proceed to the next step of artificially incubating them.

With wet hands, gently hold the brooding female in one hand. With a pencil in the other, carefully pry open its mouth over the parents' aquarium with a net in place. After the juveniles have been released from the female's mouth, the babies can be transferred to a grow-out aquarium.

PARENTS

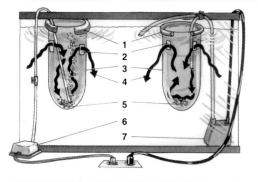

Two types of artificial incubators for mouthbrooding cichlid eggs.

1. flotation device
2. vents
3. inverted plastic soda bottle
4. water current
5. embryo eggs
6. air pump
7. water pump

Artificial Incubation

A typical incubator for mouthbrooding cichlid eggs or embryos consists of a small container setup inside an aquarium that, by means of aeration or gentle current, keeps the eggs in constant motion, permitting the proper development of the eggs or embryos into free-swimming juveniles. The container should be clear so that you can monitor the development of the embryos. After you have stripped the female of her clutch, the eggs or embryos should immediately be placed into the incubator. You will be able to ascertain when they become free-swimming when they have absorbed their yolk sacs and look like tiny fishes. Once they have reached this stage, they can be released from the incubator. You may want to place the incubator inside the grow-out aquarium in order to minimize the stress of transferring the juveniles to it.

If you wish to set up the artificial incubator in the grow-out aquarium, it should have the same water conditions and temperature as that of the parents' aquarium so that the eggs or embryos will not have to adjust to any change in water quality or temperature during their transfer and will not go into shock from the initial move. The grow-out aquarium (a 10-gallon [38 L] aquarium is ideal) should not have any decorations or gravel.

A sponge filter should be used, since it will not ensnare the juveniles. It provides adequate biological filtration, but you must remember that it will need between four and seven weeks to cycle and function properly before the juveniles are placed in the aquarium.

A REPRESENTATIVE SELECTION OF LAKE MALAWI CICHLIDS

Since there are around 800 species of Lake Malawi cichlids known, to cover such a vast number of species in a single volume would require a book many times the size of this introductory guide. My aim, therefore, is to cover those species that are commonly encountered in the trade, as well as a few rare species and new imports that have graced the hobby in the past few years. Every effort has been made to properly identify the species in this section, but, due to ever-changing taxonomic perspectives on these cichlids, there may be names that not all ichthyologists or hobbyists will agree upon. For example, there is some controversy regarding the splitting up of the mbuna genus *Pseudotropheus*. Some strongly feel that the zebras should reside in the genus *Maylandia*, while others feel that they belong to the genus *Metriaclima*, a genus erected as a replacement name for the vaguely described genus *Maylandia*. Both sides give their reasons, but since the justification given thus far to use the genus *Metriaclima* outweighs the reasons given for using the genus *Maylandia*, I have opted to use the genus *Metriaclima* for this well-known group of Malawi cichlids. The

genus *Pseudotropheus* is in a state of taxonomic flux, and new genera will be erected in the coming years to encompass those species that currently make up natural groupings, such as the Elongatus Group, the Aggressive Group, the Variable Group, and so on.

If there is some question as to the identity of a particular species, the designation "cf." before the species name will indicate that the cichlid in question is closely related to or is probably the species for which the scientific name is being applied. Any genus name with quotes indicates that the species will likely be placed into a newly erected genus upon further scientific analysis. The cichlids of Lake Malawi are referred to in the hobby largely by their scientific name, and to a lesser extent, their common name. The use of scientific names is necessary, and whenever a species is also known by one or more common names, such name(s) will follow the current scientific name. Invalid or misapplied scientific names are also listed in this part when applicable.

Since most Lake Malawi cichlids maintained in the hobby belong to the Haplochromis group and Mbuna group within the Haplochromine category, the species covered in this chapter will be from these two groups. The Mbuna group will be covered first, followed by the Haplochromis group, both alphabetically

Top: Pictured is a dominant male **Cynotilapia** **afra** *from Likoma Island. Bottom: Pictured is a mutation of* **Labeotropheus** **trewavasae** *from Thumbi West Island.*

A male **Cynotilapia afra** *from Cobue, Mozambique.*

This color variant of C. afra *from Likoma Island is one of the more striking races.*

by genus. A brief discussion is included for all the species covered. Information is presented on the name, location and natural habitat, adult size, husbandry requirements, diet, and the breeding of each species.

The Mbuna Group

Name: *Cynotilapia afra*

Location and Natural Habitat: Found in the northern third of the lake, as well as along the east coast near the Mozambique/Malawi border. Inhabits shallow rocky areas.

Adult Size: To 4 inches (10 cm).

Husbandry Requirements: Should be maintained in groups of six to ten. A moderately aggressive species. Will need an aquarium no smaller than 50 gallons (200 L) with plenty of rocks piled up to form caves and passageways. Can be kept in a community setup so long as the other aquarium inhabitants are not overly aggressive.

Diet: Algae and plankton in the wild. Offer a variety of aquarium foods. Diet should be supplemented with spirulina flakes and live baby brine shrimp.

Breeding: A maternal mouthbrooder. Males establish territories among the rocks, and spawning occurs within the rocks of the male's territory. Brooding females will join with the other females in the open. Feed juveniles live baby brine shrimp and finely crushed spirulina flakes.

Name: *Genyochromis mento,* **Malawi Scale Eater**

Location and Natural Habitat: Found throughout the lake, in sandy and well as rocky habitats. Its color pattern is often similar to the colors of the surrounding habitat as well as to neighboring mbuna species.

Adult Size: To 5 inches (12.5 cm).

Pictured is an orange-blotched (OB) color variant of **Genyochromis mento** *from Thumbi West Island.*

Husbandry Requirements: Wild imports should be maintained by themselves until they can be weaned over to commercially prepared aquarium foods. Once acclimated, they are considered to be somewhat timid to fishes of equal size or larger. Provide plenty of rocks in the form of caves and passageways. Aquarium size should be no smaller than 50 gallons (200 L).

Diet: The scales and fins of other cichlids in the wild. May take some time to be weaned onto prepared aquarium foods. Initially, one may need to provide unwanted cichlids as a source of scales during the transition stage.

Breeding: Maternal mouthbrooder. Spawning takes place in the open. After spawning, the male should be removed, and the brooding female allowed to incubate her brood to full term without being molested. Feed juveniles finely crushed flake food.

Name: *Iodotropheus sprengerae,* **Rusty Cichlid**

Location and Natural Habitat: Found only in Chinyankwazi and Chinyamwezi Islands in the southeast arm of the lake. These islands consist exclusively of rocks.

Adult Size: To 3¹/₂ inches (8.5 cm).

Husbandry Requirements: A peaceful, non-territorial mbuna outside of reproductive periods. Can be maintained in aquariums as small as 25 gallons (90 L). Provide plenty of rocks in the form of caves and passageways. Not to be kept with larger, highly aggressive species.

Diet: Omnivorous in the wild. Offer a wide variety of commercially prepared aquarium foods.

Breeding: Spawning takes place among the rocks. Brooding females can be maintained together in the same aquarium as the spawn-

The Rusty Cichlid, **Iodotropheus sprengerae,** *is an ideal beginner's mbuna.*

ing male. Provide rocks as refuge for juveniles. Feed live baby brine shrimp to the juveniles.

Name: *Labeotropheus fuelleborni*

Location and Natural Habitat: Found throughout the lake in water no deeper than 25 feet (7.5 m) in rocky habitats. Occurs in a wide variety of geographic color variations throughout the lake.

Adult Size: To 7 inches (17.5 cm).

Husbandry Requirements: A large, robust species that will need a relatively large aquarium

Pictured is an orange-blotched (OB) **Labeotropheus fuelleborni** *from Maleri Island.*

This variant of **Labeotropheus fuelleborni** *is from Katale Island, Malawi.*

Pictured is an orange female **Labeotropheus trewavasae** *from Thumbi West Island.*

This **Labeotropheus trewavasae** *hails from Manda, Tanzania.*

of at least 75 gallons (300 L). Provide plenty of rocks in the form of caves and passageways. Maintain only with other similar-sized, aggressive species that can hold their own against this domineering species.

Diet: Algae on rocks in the wild. Offer a variety of commercially prepared aquarium foods high in spirulina or algae.

Breeding: Male becomes highly aggressive toward the other aquarium residents during spawning. Provide ample hiding places for brooding females to retreat to; otherwise, remove the male to allow the female to brood her clutch of eggs unmolested. Feed juveniles live baby brine shrimp and finely ground spirulina flake food.

Name: *Labeotropheus trewavasae*
Location and Natural Habitat: Found throughout the lake, from the surface to a depth of around 100 feet (30 m) in rocky habitats. Occurs in a wide variety of geographic color variations throughout the lake.

Adult Size: To 6 inches (15 cm).

Husbandry Requirements: A slender, less hardy species than the other species of the

Pictured is a male **Labeotropheus trewavasae** *from Thumbi West Island.*

genus. Aquarium should be no smaller than 50 gallons (200 L). Provide plenty of rocks in the form of caves and passageways. Is easily bullied by more aggressive species.

Diet: Algae on rocks in the wild. Offer a variety of commercially prepared aquarium foods high in spirulina or algae.

Breeding: Male becomes aggressive toward the other aquarium residents that approach the spawning site. Provide hiding places for brooding females to retreat. The male need not be removed provided there are ample hiding places for the female. Feed juveniles live baby brine shrimp and finely ground spirulina flake food.

Name: *Labidochromis caeruleus*, **Electric Yellow, Pearl Labidochromis**

Location and Natural Habitat: Found only on the west coast between Ruarwe and Nkhata Bay, and on the east coast in southern Tanzania to northern Mozambique waters. Inhabits the deeper rocky regions at a depth of 35 to 100 feet (10–30 m). Occurs in various shades of white or yellow depending on location.

Adult Size: To 3 inches (7.5 cm).

Pictured is a color variant of **Labidochromis caeruleus** *from Lion's Cove, Malawi.*

Husbandry Requirements: A small, peaceful mbuna that can be maintained in aquariums as small as 25 gallons (90 L). Provide plenty of rocks in the form of caves and passageways. Do not maintain with large, aggressive mbuna. Best maintained in small groups of around six individuals.

Diet: Small aquatic invertebrates living on rocks in the wild. Offer a wide variety of commercially prepared aquarium foods. The yellow race (pictured here) should be fed carotene-rich foods to help maintain its brilliant yellow coloration.

Breeding: A nonterritorial species. Spawning will occur anywhere in the aquarium. Male and female can be maintained together after spawning, without the female being unduly harassed. Feed juveniles of the yellow race predominantly live baby brine shrimp for at least their first two months.

Name: *Labidochromis* sp. **Mbamba Bay**

Location and Natural Habitat: Found at Mbamba Bay (Ngkuyo) Island in Tanzania and along the nearby coastline.

Adult Size: To 3½ inches (8.5 cm).

Labidochromis *sp. Mbamba Bay sports a color pattern strongly reminiscent of some* **Cynotilapia** *species.*

Husbandry Requirements: A secretive species that will require plenty of rocks piled up to form caves and passageways. Aquarium should be at least 50 gallons (200 L). Do not maintain with larger, more aggressive species of the Mbuna group.

Diet: Tiny invertebrates hidden in the rocks. Offer a wide variety of commercially prepared aquarium foods. Supplement the diet with live baby brine shrimp and daphnia.

Breeding: Spawning takes place deep inside the male's cave. The ovigerous female will stay hidden for the duration of brooding period. Feed juveniles live baby brine shrimp and finely crushed flake food.

Name: *Labidochromis* sp. **Perlmutt**

Location and Natural Habitat: Found primarily at Mbamba Bay, Tanzania. It lives among large rocks at a depth ranging from 35 to 150 feet (10–45 m).

Adult Size: To 3½ inches (7.5 cm).

Husbandry Requirements: A small, peaceful mbuna that can be maintained in aquariums as small as 25 gallons (90 L). Provide plenty of

The name Perlmutt is German for Mother-of-Pearl, an apt name for this Labidochromis species.

rocks in the form of caves and passageways. Do not maintain with large, aggressive mbuna. Best maintained in small groups of around six individuals.

Diet: Small aquatic invertebrates living on rocks in the wild. Offer a wide variety of commercially prepared aquarium foods.

Breeding: A nonterritorial species. Spawning will occur anywhere in the aquarium. Male and female can be maintained together after spawning, and the female can brood her clutch of eggs unmolested. Feed juveniles live baby brine shrimp and finely crushed flake food.

Name: *Melanochromis auratus*

Location and Natural Habitat: Found in the southern third of the lake, over rocky habitats.

Adult Size: To 3½ inches (9 cm).

Husbandry Requirements: A very active and moderately aggressive mbuna that will need plenty of space. An aquarium no smaller than 50 gallons (200 L) is recommended. Provide plenty of rocks in the form of caves and passageways. Maintain only with other aggressive mbuna species.

Diet: Algae and small aquatic invertebrates living within the algae in the wild. Will accept all kinds of commercially prepared aquarium foods. Supplement the diet with spirulina flakes and algae wafers.

Breeding: A precocious species. Spawning will usually take place among the rocks of the male's territory with the male and female circling each other vigorously before eggs are laid. The male can be removed after spawning, or the female removed to a smaller, quiet, and secluded aquarium to brood her eggs to full term. Feed juveniles live baby brine shrimp and finely crushed flake food.

A male **Melanochromis auratus** *from Mbenji Island.*

Juvenile and female **Melanochromis auratus** *display yellow, white, and black banding.*

Name: *Melanochromis baliodigma*, **Melanochromis Blotch**

Location and Natural Habitat: Found along the Mozambique shoreline as well as Chizumulu and Likoma Island. Inhabits the regions where the rocks and sand meet.

Adult Size: To 4 inches (10 cm).

Husbandry Requirements: An active, moderately aggressive opportunistic mbuna. Best maintained in a community aquarium of other similarly aggressive mbuna. Aquarium should be no smaller than 75 gallons (300 L). Provide plenty of rocks in the form of caves and passageways.

Diet: Piscivorous in the wild, feeding on juvenile cichlids. Adapts readily to commercially prepared aquarium foods. High-protein foods should dominate the diet.

Breeding: Secretive cave spawner. Provide sufficient rocks, not only for spawning activity, but for the brooding female to find a secluded area to brood her clutch. Feed juveniles live baby brine shrimp and finely ground flake foods.

Name: *Melanochromis johannii*

Location and Natural Habitat: Found on the east coast between Masinje in Malawi northward to Metangula in Mozambique. Inhabits the regions where the rocks and sand meet.

Adult Size: To 4 inches (10 cm).

Husbandry Requirements: A very active and moderately aggressive mbuna that will need plenty of space. Provide plenty of rocks in the form of caves and passageways. Best maintained as a group with at least eight individuals.

Melanochromis baliodigma, *from the east coast of Malawi at Masinje, is piscivorous.*

This male Melanochromis johanni *from Masinje displays sharp horizontal barring.*

"Melanochromis" labrosus *will undoubtedly be placed into a genus of its own.*

An aquarium no smaller than 50 gallons (200 L) is recommended. Provide plenty of rocks in the form of caves and passageways.

Diet: Omnivorous in the wild. Offer a wide variety of commercially prepared aquarium foods.

Breeding: The male will spawn within his territory in the rocks. Provided there are plenty of hiding places, and many females to distract the male, the brooding female need not be removed. Feed juveniles live baby brine shrimp in order to maintain the integrity of their intense yellow/orange coloration.

Name: *"Melanochromis" labrosus*
Location and Natural Habitat: Found throughout the lake wherever rocks are present. A rarely seen species.

Adult Size: To 6 inches (15 cm).

Husbandry Requirements: A nonterritorial species that is ideally suited to a Malawi cichlid community aquarium. Provide plenty of rocks piled up to form caves and passageways. Aquarium should be no smaller than 50 gallons (200 L).

Diet: Juvenile cichlids in the wild. Adapts readily to commercially prepared aquarium foods. High-protein foods should dominate the diet.

Breeding: Spawning will occur hidden away among the rocks, and the brooding female need not be removed from the aquarium provided there are sufficient hiding places. Feed juveniles live baby brine shrimp and finely crushed flake foods.

Name: *Melanochromis lepidiadaptes,*
Melanochromis lepidophage
Location and Natural Habitat: Found only at West Reef and Eccles Reef in the northern part of the southeast arm of the lake. Inhabits the rocks at these reefs.

Adult Size: To 4 inches (10 cm).

Husbandry Requirements: An active scavenging species that will need a large aquarium of at least 75 gallons (300 L). Provide plenty of rocks piled up to form caves and passageways. Can be kept with other larger species of the Haplochromis or Mbuna group.

Diet: Omnivorous. It has also been known to consume the scales of other cichlids. The scale-eating tendency is rarely observed in captive specimens. Offer a wide variety of commercially prepared aquarium fish foods.

Breeding: The male will spawn within his territory in the rocks. Maintain several females with the male, so that it will not focus its aggression on any one female. Feed juveniles live baby brine shrimp and finely crushed flake food.

Name: *Melanochromis vermivorus*
Location and Natural Habitat: Found in the southwest region of the lake, including Cape Maclear peninsula, wherever extensive rocky habitats are present.

Adult Size: To 4 inches (10 cm).

Husbandry Requirements: A very active and moderately aggressive mbuna that will need an aquarium no smaller than 75 gallons (300 L). Provide plenty of rocks in the form of caves and passageways. Best maintained as a group of at least ten. Do not maintain with other similar-looking *Melanochromis* species, as accidental hybridization may occur.

Diet: Omnivorous in the wild. Offer a wide variety of commercially prepared aquarium foods.

In the wild, **Melanochromis lepidadaptes** *occasionally consumes the scales of other cichlids.*

Breeding: The male will spawn within his territory in the rocks. Provided there are ample hiding places and many females to distract the male, brooding females need not be removed. Feed juveniles live baby brine shrimp and finely crushed flake food.

Name: *Metriaclima aurora*
Location and Natural Habitat: Found in shallow water at Likoma Island where the rocks and sand meet. Most numerous on the east side of the island. Has been transplanted to

Pictured is a male **Melanochromis vermivorus** *from Thumbi West Island.*

Metriaclima aurora *from Thumbi West Island.*

Thumbi West Island in Cape Maclear National Park.

Adult Size: To 4 inches (10 cm).

Husbandry Requirements: A relatively mild-mannered species. Digs profusely; therefore, gravel or sand should be kept to a minimum. Avoid using an undergravel filter. Provide plenty of rocks in the form of caves and passageways. Aquarium should be at least 50 gallons (200 L).

Diet: Algae from the rocks in the wild. Offer commercially prepared aquarium foods high in spirulina or algae.

Breeding: A secretive cave spawner. Provide sufficient rocks so that the brooding female can find a secluded area to brood her eggs. Feed juveniles live baby brine shrimp and finely ground flake foods.

Name: *Metriaclima barlowi,* **Golden Zebra**
Location and Natural Habitat: Found throughout the southern portion of the lake where islands are present and where the rocks and sand meet.

Adult Size: To 5 inches (12.5 cm).

Husbandry Requirements: A highly aggres-

sive mbuna. A large aquarium (100 gallons [400 L]) minimum, with plenty of rocks is recommended. Maintain only with other aggressive species.

Diet: Algae from the rocks in the wild. Offer commercially prepared aquarium foods high in spirulina or algae.

Breeding: A secretive cave spawner. The male can often be highly aggressive during spawning. After spawning, the brooding female should be removed to another aquarium. Feed juveniles live baby brine shrimp as a first food.

Name: *Metriaclima callainos,* **Cobalt Zebra**
Location and Natural Habitat: Found primarily at Nkhata Bay as well as in the northeast from Ikombe to Puulu in Tanzania over rocky habitats from shallow water to a depth of at least 80 feet (25 m). Has been transplanted to Cape Maclear National Park.

Adult Size: To 5 inches (12.5 cm).

Husbandry Requirements: A mildly aggressive species that should be maintained in groups of eight to twelve. The aquarium should be at least 75 gallons (300 L) and there should be plenty of rocks piled up to form caves and

This **Metriaclima barlowi** *from Mbenji Island is an aggressive mbuna species.*

Pictured is a male Cobalt Blue Zebra (**Metriaclima callaninos**) *from Nkhata Bay.*

passageways. Can be kept with smaller, less aggressive mbuna.

Diet: Algae on rocks as well as plankton in the wild. Offer a wide variety of commercially prepared aquarium fish foods. A majority of the diet should be spirulina- or algae-based.

Breeding: The dominant male tends to be more aggressive during periods of sexual activity. Females are only tolerated within the male's territory for spawning. After spawning, the brooding female will join with the other females in the open. This behavior will be encouraged if several females and a single male are maintained together. As a first food, feed juveniles live baby brine shrimp.

Name: *Metriaclima crabro*, **Bumble Bee**

Location and Natural Habitat: Found throughout the lake over rocky habitats from shallow to deep water.

Adult Size: 4½ inches (11 cm).

Husbandry Requirements: A relatively peaceful, active mbuna. Aquarium should be at least 50 gallons (200 L) with plenty of rocks. Interacts well with most mbuna, provided they are not too aggressive.

Diet: Omnivorous, but also feeds on the parasites of the large catfish, *Bagrus meridionalis*, as well as its eggs. In captivity, adapts readily to commercially prepared aquarium foods. Feed high-protein foods such as fresh shrimp and ocean plankton.

Breeding: Spawning males darken considerably. A secretive cave spawner, adequate refuge should be present for the female to retire to in order to brood her clutch of eggs unmolested. As a first food for the juveniles, feed live baby brine shrimp and finely crushed flakes.

Name: *Metriaclima estherae*, **Red Zebra**

Location and Natural Habitat: Irregularly distributed from Metangula and Minos Reef in Mozambique southward to Gome in Malawi. Found only in rocky areas.

Adult Size: To 4½ inches (11.5 cm).

Husbandry Requirements: A very active species that will need a large aquarium of at least 75 gallons (300 L). Provide plenty of rocks in the form of caves and passageways. Do not maintain with other similar-looking species, such as *Metriaclima callainos*, Cobalt Zebra, since hybridization is likely to occur.

The Bumble Bee, **Metriaclima crabro,** *is known for its odd dining habits.*

This orange color mutation of the female Red Zebra, **M. estherae,** *is most desirable.*

Diet: Algae from the rocks in the wild. Feed commercially prepared foods such as spirulina flakes and algae wafers.

Breeding: The dominant male vigorously defends his spawning site. After spawning, the female may retreat to a secluded place, or join with the other females out in the open. This brood/shoaling behavior will be seen if several females to a single male are maintained together in a large aquarium. As a first food, feed juveniles live baby brine shrimp.

A male **Metriaclima lombardoi** *from Mbenji Island.*

This female **M. lombardoi** *displays a striking dark and light blue contrast.*

Name: *Metriaclima lombardoi,* **Kenyi**
Location and Natural Habitat: Found at Mbenji Island and nearby Nkomo Reef. Inhabits the rock/sand interface down to 100 feet (30 m).
Adult Size: To 5 inches (12.5 cm).
Husbandry Requirements: Wild-caught specimens are highly aggressive, while captive-bred specimens several generations removed from the wild are significantly more amiable. Nevertheless, a large aquarium (minimum 75 gallons [300 L]) is recommended. Provide plenty of rocks in the form of caves and passageways. Do not house with less aggressive mbuna such as those of the genus *Labidochromis.*

Diet: Algae on rocks as well as plankton in the wild. Feed a wide variety of commercially prepared aquarium fish foods. A majority of the diet should consist of spirulina flakes or algae wafers.

Breeding: Dominant males are extremely aggressive, and unless you maintain a large number of males and females together, it is advisable to remove the brooding females to a more secluded aquarium so that they can brood their eggs unmolested to full term. Feed juveniles live baby brine shrimp and finely crushed flake food.

Name: *Metriaclima mbenjii,* **Red Top Cobalt Zebra**
Location and Natural Habitat: Endemic to Mbenji Island in the upper 40 feet (13 m) of water in rocky areas.
Adult Size: To 5½ inches (13.5 cm).
Husbandry Requirements: A very active species that will need a large aquarium of at least 75 gallons (300 L). Provide plenty of rocks

The Red Top Cobalt Zebra was recently described as Metriaclima mbenjii.

The Red Top BB (black bar) Zebra has been described as Metriaclima pyrsonotus.

in the form of caves and passageways. Do not maintain with the nearly identical *Metriaclima greshakei*, since hybridization is likely to occur.

Diet: Algae on rocks as well as plankton in the wild. Feed a wide variety of commercially prepared aquarium fish foods. A majority of the diet should consist of spirulina flakes or algae wafers.

Breeding: The dominant male vigorously defends his spawning site. After spawning, the female may retreat to a secluded place, or join with the other females in the open. As a first food, feed juveniles live baby brine shrimp and finely crushed flake food.

Name: *Metriaclima pyrsonotus*, **Red Top BB Zebra**

Location and Natural Habitat: Found only at Nakantenga Island over heavily silted rocks. Occurs predominantly at the northern tip of the island at a depth between 10 to 90 feet (3–27 m).

Adult Size: To 5 inches (12.5 cm).

Husbandry Requirements: An active species that will need a large aquarium of at least 75 gallons (300 L). Provide plenty of rocks in the

The extremely rare orange color mutation of M. pyrsonotus *only occurs in the male sex.*

form of caves and passageways. Do not maintain with *Metriaclima zebra*, since hybridization is likely to occur.

Diet: Algae on rocks as well as plankton in the wild. Feed a wide variety of commercially prepared aquarium fish foods. A majority of the diet should consist of spirulina flakes or algae wafers.

Breeding: The dominant male defends his spawning site and coaxes any receptive female to spawn. After spawning, the brooding female

This male BB (black bar) **Metriaclima** **zebra** *is from Thumbi West Island.*

Pictured is a male marmalade cat **M. zebra** *from Likoma Island.*

will join with the other females in the open. As a first food, feed juveniles live baby brine shrimp and finely crushed flake food.

Name: *Metriaclima zebra,* **Zebra**
Location and Natural Habitat: Found throughout the lake wherever rocks are present in water no deeper than 50 feet (15 m).
Adult Size: To 5 inches (12.5 cm).
Husbandry Requirements: An active species that will need an aquarium of at least 75 gallons (300 L). Provide plenty of rocks in the form of caves and passageways. Do not main-

tain with *Metriaclima pyrsonotus,* since hybridization is likely to occur.
Diet: Algae on rocks as well as plankton in the wild. Offer a wide variety of commercially prepared aquarium fish foods. Supplement the diet with spirulina flakes or algae wafers.
Breeding: The dominant male defends his spawning site and coaxes any receptive female to spawn. After spawning, the female may retreat to a secluded place, or join with the other females in the open. Feed juveniles live baby brine shrimp and finely crushed flake food.

Name: *Petrotilapia chrysos,* **Gold Petrotilapia**
Location and Natural Habitat: Found at Chinyamwezi and Chinyankwazi Islands.
Adult Size: To 6 inches (15 cm).
Husbandry Requirements: An aggressive species best maintained in an aquarium with a minimum size of 75 gallons (300 L). Provide plenty of rocks in the form of caves and passageways. Can be kept with other aggressive mbuna. Do not maintain with any Malawi cichlids from the Haplochromis group.

A female **Petrotilapia chrysos** *from Chinyamwezi and Chinyankwazi islands.*

Diet: Algae on the rocks in the wild. Offer commercially prepared aquarium foods such as spirulina flakes and algae wafers.

Breeding: Maintain several females to a single male. The male will court any receptive female, and afterwards the female will find a secluded place to brood her eggs. Feed live baby brine shrimp along with finely crushed spirulina flake food.

Name: *Petrotilapia* sp. **Small Blue**

Location and Natural Habitat: Found around the general vicinity of Nkhata Bay at a minimum depth of 30 feet (9 m) over rocky areas.

Adult Size: To 7 inches (18 cm).

Husbandry Requirements: A large, aggressive, and solitary species that will need an aquarium of at least 100 gallons (400 L). Best maintained in a community aquarium with other aggressive mbuna. Provide plenty of rocks in the form of caves and passageways.

Diet: Algae on the rocks in the wild. Offer commercially prepared aquarium foods such as spirulina flakes and algae wafers.

Breeding: Males will harass unreceptive females. If a female cannot be maintained in

Pictured are young male and female of **Petrotilapia** *sp.* **Small Blue of Nkhata Bay.**

the same aquarium as the male, try the divider method. Place a single male on one side of the divider (firmly secured egg crate), and a single female on the other side. Spawning should take place between the vented divider, then the brooding female can incubate her brood unmolested. Feed live baby brine shrimp along with finely crushed spirulina flake food.

Name: *Pseudotropheus cyaneus*

Location and Natural Habitat: Endemic to Chinyamwezi Island. Lives in close contact to the rocks.

Adult Size: 3½ inches (8 cm).

Husbandry Requirements: A moderately aggressive species that is best maintained in groups of six to ten in an aquarium no smaller than 50 gallons (200 L). Provide plenty of rocks in the form of caves and passageways.

Diet: Feeds on small aquatic invertebrates living within the rocks in the wild. Offer a wide variety of commercially prepared aquarium foods.

Breeding: A secretive spawner. Spawning takes place hidden in the male's cavelike terri-

Pseudotropheus cyaneus *is endemic to* **Chinyamwezi Island.**

Pseudotropheus demasoni is a mbuna species where male and female share the same color pattern.

This male **Pseudotropheus flavus** *was photographed at Chinyankwazi Island.*

tory. Afterwards, the brooding female will find a secluded place to brood her eggs undisturbed. Feed newly released juveniles live baby brine shrimp.

Name: *Pseudotropheus demasoni*
Location and Natural Habitat: Found at Pombo Rocks and nearby Ndumbi Point in shallow, rocky environs.
Adult Size: To 2³/₄ inches (7 cm).
Husbandry Requirements: A mild-mannered, tiny mbuna that is best maintained in groups of six to ten. Aquarium should be at least 30 gallons (120 L). Provide several large rocks to form caves and passageways. Can be maintained with larger Malawi cichlids from the Haplochromis group provided they have sufficient refuge.
Diet: Algae on the rocks in the wild. Offer commercially prepared aquarium foods such as spirulina flakes and algae wafers.
Breeding: Male will spawn in the most secluded area of the aquarium. Brooding females can be kept with the male without being overly harassed. Feed juveniles live baby

brine shrimp and finely crushed spirulina flake food.

Name: *Pseudotropheus flavus,* **Dinghani**
Location and Natural Habitat: Endemic to Chinyankwazi Island. Lives in close contact to the rocks.
Adult Size: To 3¹/₂ inches (8 cm).
Husbandry Requirements: Outside of periods of sexual activity, a mild-mannered mbuna that is best maintained in groups of six to ten. Aquarium should be at least 50 gallons (200 L). Provide plenty of rocks to form caves and passageways.
Diet: Omnivorous in the wild. Offer a variety of commercially prepared aquarium foods. Emphasis should be placed on those foods high in carotene in order to maintain the integrity of the orange pigment.
Breeding: Males become highly aggressive within their territories during spawning. As long as the aquarium is sufficiently large, brooding females need not be removed. Feed juveniles live baby brine shrimp as a first food.

Left: Quality **Pseudotropheus saulosi** *males display prominent vertical barring. Right: Pictured is a female* **Pseudotropheus saulosi** *photographed at Taiwan Reef.*

Name: *Pseudotropheus saulosi*

Location and Natural Habitat: Endemic to Taiwan Reef, just north of Chizumulu Island. Habitat consists of large boulders piled up to within 30 feet (9 m) of the surface. Strong current often sweeps through the reef.

Adult Size: To 3 inches (7.5 cm).

Husbandry Requirements: A relatively peaceful mbuna. Best maintained in groups of ten, in aquarium no smaller than 50 gallons (200 L). Provide plenty of rocks piled up to form caves and passageways.

Diet: Algae and small aquatic invertebrates living on the rocks in the wild. Will accept a wide variety of prepared aquarium foods. Supplement the diet with spirulina flakes or algae wafers.

Breeding: Dominant males stake out territories, while the females scurry about in large schools hugging the surface of large boulders. Several females to each male is recommended. After spawning, the brooding female will join with other females to incubate her eggs. Feed juveniles live baby brine shrimp.

Name: *Pseudotropheus socolofi,* **Pindani**

Location and Natural Habitat: Found along the Mozambique coast just south of Likoma Island down to Tumbi Point, wherever there is an even mixture of rocks and sand.

Adult Size: 3 inches (7.5 cm).

Husbandry Requirements: A mildly aggressive mbuna that should be maintained in an aquarium no smaller than 30 gallons (120 L) with plenty of rocks. Can be maintained with less aggressive species from the genus *Labidochromis.* Avoid maintaining with highly aggressive mbuna species.

Diet: Omnivorous in the wild. Feed a wide variety of commercially prepared aquarium foods.

Pseudotropheus socolofi *is a common species in the aquarium trade.*

Breeding: The dominant male will be somewhat larger and more aggressive than the female. Spawning takes place in seclusion and the female will usually brood her eggs hidden away among the rocks. Feed juveniles live baby brine shrimp and finely crushed flakes.

Name: *Pseudotropheus* sp. **Acei**
Location and Natural Habitat: Found on the west coast from Ngara to Senga Bay. Inhabits shallow sandy areas wherever submerged tree trunks are present.
Adult Size: To 4¹/₂ inches (11.5 cm).
Husbandry Requirements: A peaceful, weakly territorial species that is best maintained with other nonaggressive species. Provide pieces of driftwood and a few smooth stones over a shallow layer of silica sand. Best maintained in groups of ten in an aquarium no smaller than 50 gallons (200 L).
Diet: Invertebrates and algae on submerged tree trunks in the wild. Will accept a wide variety of prepared aquarium foods.
Breeding: Spawning takes place anywhere over the sand. Brooding females will congregate with the other females and subdominant males. Feed newly released juveniles live baby brine shrimp and finely crushed flake foods.

Name: *Pseudotropheus* sp. **Chewere Elongatus**
Location and Natural Habitat: Found 3 miles (5 km) north of Chilumba at Chewere. Inhabits the area where the rocks and sand intermingle.
Adult Size: To 4 inches (10 cm).
Husbandry Requirements: An aggressive species that is best maintained in groups of 15. Provide plenty of rocks piled up to form caves and passageways. Use no smaller than a 75-gallon (300 L) aquarium.
Diet: Algae and plankton in the wild. Offer a varied diet of commercially prepared aquarium foods. Supplement the diet with spirulina flakes or algae wafers.
Breeding: Spawning males are very territorial and aggressive. Provide enough hiding places for the females to avoid the aggressive tendencies of the male. Receptive females will be allowed in the male's territory long enough to spawn. Afterwards, the female will retreat to a quiet place to brood her eggs. Feed juveniles

The yellow-tailed variant of **Pseudotropheus** *sp.* **Acei** *is found in Nkhata Bay.*

Pseudotropheus *sp.* **Chewere Elongatus** *is found at Chewere, just north of Chilumba.*

This Pseudotropheus *sp. Masimbwe Elongatus comes from Masimbwe and Likoma islands.*

Pseudotropheus *sp. Msobo is endemic to much of the Tanzanian coastline. Pictured is a male from Magunga.*

live baby brine shrimp and finely crushed flake foods.

Name: *Pseudotropheus* sp. **Masimbwe Elongatus**

Location and Natural Habitat: Found at Likoma Island wherever rocks are present. Particularly plentiful at the small rocky island of Masimbwe located one mile (1.4 km) south of Likoma Island.

Adult Size: To 4 inches (10 cm).

Husbandry Requirements: An aggressive mbuna that will need an aquarium of at least 75 gallons (300 L) with plenty of rocks piled up to form caves and passageways. Males are highly territorial and will often spar with other males if the aquarium is too small.

Diet: Small aquatic invertebrates living within the rocks in the wild. Will accept a wide variety of prepared aquarium foods.

Breeding: During spawning, the male becomes quite aggressive within his territory. As long as the aquarium is sufficiently large, brooding females need not be removed. Feed juveniles live baby brine shrimp as a first food.

Pictured is a female Pseudotropheus *sp. Msobo from Magunga.*

Name: *Pseudotropheus* sp. **Msobo**

Location and Natural Habitat: Found on the Tanzanian coast from Cape Kaiser southward to Lundu at depths of 15 to 100 feet (5 to 30 m). Inhabits rocky areas exclusively.

Adult Size: To 4 inches (10 cm).

Husbandry Requirements: Small groups of no fewer than six individuals should be housed in aquariums of 50 gallons (200 L) with several rocks piled up to form caves and passageways.

Pseudotropheus sp. *Red Top Ndumbi is endemic to Ndumbi Reef.*

Tropheops gracilior's range mostly lies within Cape Maclear National Park.

Diet: Plankton and algae in the wild. Offer a variety of commercially prepared aquarium foods. Supplement the diet with spirulina flakes and algae wafers.

Breeding: The male will aggressively stake out a territory to defend and for spawning. After spawning, the brooding female will retreat to a secluded area of the aquarium. Feed newly released juveniles live baby brine shrimp and finely crushed flake foods.

Name: *Pseudotropheus* sp. **Red Top Ndumbi**
Location and Natural Habitat: Found only at Ndumbi Reef in Tanzanian waters at a depth of 15 to 26 feet (5 to 8 m).
Adult Size: To 3 inches (7.5 cm).
Husbandry Requirements: A peaceful, small mbuna that can be housed in aquariums as small as 20 gallons (80 L). To provide a more secure environment for this timid species, furnish rocks piled up to form hiding places and passageways.
Diet: Algae on the rocks in the wild. Offer commercially prepared foods such as spirulina flakes and algae wafers.

Breeding: Spawning will take place hidden in the rocks. Afterwards the female can be left with the male and other females to brood her eggs. Feed newly released juveniles live baby brine shrimp and finely crushed spirulina flakes.

Name: *Tropheops gracilior*
Location and Natural Habitat: Found at Cape Maclear and the surrounding islands. Inhabits rocky areas at depths of 15 to 50 feet (3–15 m).
Adult Size: To 4 inches (10 cm).
Husbandry Requirements: An aggressive species that is best maintained in a community aquarium of similarly aggressive species. Aquarium should be no smaller than 75 gallons (300 L) with plenty of rocks.
Diet: Algae on the rocks in the wild. Offer commercially prepared foods such as spirulina flakes and algae wafers.
Breeding: Males can harass females, so it is best to remove the female to another aquarium, or remove the male from the spawning aquarium and permit the female to brood her

eggs unmolested. Feed newly released juveniles live baby brine shrimp and finely crushed spirulina flakes.

Name: *Tropheops tropheops*
Location and Natural Habitat: Found at Cape Maclear and southward wherever rocky habitats are present at a depth of 3 feet to 80 feet (1–24 m).
Adult Size: To 4½ inches (11 cm).
Husbandry Requirements: A moderately aggressive species that needs plenty of space. Aquarium should be no smaller than 75 gallons (300 L) with plenty of rocks.
Diet: Algae on the rocks in the wild. Offer commercially prepared foods such as spirulina flakes and algae wafers.
Breeding: Best maintained in groups of eight to ten. Spawning takes place within the males' territory. Afterwards, the brooding female will retreat to a secluded area of the aquarium. Feed newly released juveniles live baby brine shrimp and finely crushed spirulina flakes.

Name: *Tropheops* sp. **Chitande Yellow**
Location and Natural Habitat: Found in the northern regions of the lake wherever rocks and sand intermingle.
Adult Size: To 5 inches (12.5 cm).
Husbandry Requirements: A robust, aggressive species that will need to be housed in aquariums no smaller than 75 gallons (300 L). Best maintained in a colony of 12 or more individuals. Provide ample hiding places with rocks piled up to form caves and passageways.
Diet: Algae on the rocks in the wild. Offer commercially prepared foods such as spirulina flakes and algae wafers.

This variant of Tropheops tropheops *is found in shallow water at Zimbawe Rock.*

This male orange-blotched (OB) color mutation of Tropheops tropheops *was seen at Otter Island.*

Pictured is a Tropheops sp. Chitande Yellow *from Ikombe.*

Breeding: Best spawned in a group or in a mixed community of aggressive mbuna species. Spawning takes place within the male's territory. Afterwards, the brooding female will retreat to a secluded area of the aquarium. If the female is overly harassed, remove her to another aquarium so that she may brood her eggs unmolested. Feed newly released juveniles live baby brine shrimp and finely crushed spirulina flakes.

Name: *Tropheops* sp. **Red Cheek**
Location and Natural Habitat: Found at Likoma and Chizumulu Islands and the northernmost coastline of Tanzania. Particularly common in the southern region of Likoma Island wherever large boulders are present.

Adult Size: To 4 inches (10 cm).

Husbandry Requirements: An active species that should be housed in an aquarium no smaller than 50 gallons (200 L). Can be maintained with less aggressive species of the Mbuna group if plenty of hiding places are provided.

Diet: Algae on the rocks in the wild. Offer commercially prepared foods such as spirulina flakes and algae wafers.

Breeding: Males become particularly aggressive during spawning and during the defense of their spawning site. The brooding female will retreat to an area of the aquarium to brood her eggs. If the female cannot find refuge, remove her to another aquarium so that she may brood her eggs undisturbed. Feed newly released juveniles live baby brine shrimp and finely crushed spirulina flakes.

Name: *Tropheops* sp. **Red Fin**
Location and Natural Habitat: Found on the west coast in Malawi from Usisya to Chilumba, and on the east coast in Tanzania from Lundu southward into Mozambique to just north of Likoma Island. Inhabits areas with an even rock and sand combination.

Adult Size: To 4 inches (10 cm).

Husbandry Requirements: Males are solitary while females tend to form loose schools. House several females to each male. Aquarium should be a minimum of 50 gallons (200 L) with plenty of rocks piled up to form caves and passageways, as well as a shallow layer of silica sand.

Diet: Algae and aquatic invertebrates in the wild. Feed a variety of commercially prepared

The pigment on the face of **Tropheops** *sp.* **Red Cheek** *varies considerably in the wild.*

Pictured is a male **Tropheops** *sp.* **Red Fin** *from Londo, Mozambique.*

aquarium foods such as spirulina flakes and algae wafers.

Breeding: The dominant male tends to be more aggressive during periods of sexual activity. Females are tolerated within the males' territory only for spawning. After spawning the brooding female will join with the other females. This behavior is frequently observed if several females to a single male are maintained together in a large aquarium. Feed juveniles live baby brine shrimp followed by finely crushed spirulina flakes.

The Haplochromis Group

Name: *Aristochromis christyi*

Location and Natural Habitat: Found throughout the lake over sandy and rocky habitats from near the surface down to 300 feet (90 m).

Adult Size: To 14 inches (35 cm).

Husbandry Requirements: A large, predatory species that requires a large aquarium of at least 100 gallons (400 L). Males can be quite aggressive to subdominant males and females. Best maintained in groups of 12, or in a community setup with similar-sized species. Intolerant of improper water management.

Diet: Small cichlids in the wild. Offer high-protein foods such as krill, feeder guppies, and commercially prepared frozen foods.

Breeding: Maintain a single male with several females. After spawning, the female should be given a place to brood her eggs unmolested. Provide hiding places; otherwise, remove the female to a secluded aquarium. Feed newly released juveniles live baby brine shrimp and finely crushed flake foods.

Aristochromis christyi is a member of the Haplochromis group that is rare in its natural habitat.

Name: *Aulonocara hansbaenschi,* **Aulonocara nyassae, Red Shoulder Peacock**

Location and Natural Habitat: Found at the east central coastline from Cobue in Mozambique to Makanjila Point in Malawi. An introduced population exists at Thumbi West Island within Cape Maclear National Park. Inhabits the area where rocks and sand intermingle.

Adult Size: To 3½ inches (9 cm).

Husbandry Requirements: A peaceful species that can be maintained in aquariums as small as 25 gallons (90 L). Provide sufficient

Pictured is a male **Aulonocara hansbaenschi** *photographed at Thumbi West Island.*

This color variant of **Aulonocara stuart-granti,** *known as the Maulana Peacock, is found only at Chitimba Bay.*

This variant of **Aulonocara stuartgranti** *is found at Chiwindi.*

The greatest number of **Aulonocara jacobfreibergi** *variants can be found at Cape Maclear. Pictured is a male from Domwe Island.*

This variant of **A. jacobfreibergi** *was discovered at Undu Point in Tanzania, and is known as the Mamalela Peacock in the hobby.*

hiding places and a thin layer of silica sand. Can be maintained with other peaceful species from the Haplochromis and Mbuna groups. Do not maintain with any other *Aulonocara* species, as hybridization is likely to occur.

Diet: Microinvertebrates hidden in the sand and on rocks. Offer a variety of commercially prepared aquarium foods. Supplement the diet with live baby brine shrimp and daphnia.

Breeding: Maintain several females to one or two males. Spawning will take place at regular intervals, and the brooding females will join with other females in a loose aggregation. Feed newly released juveniles live baby brine shrimp.

Name: *Aulonocara stuartgranti,* **Maulana Peacock, Flavescent Peacock, Ngara Peacock, Chilumba Peacock, Blue Neon Peacock**

Location and Natural Habitat: Found throughout the northern half of the lake on the west coast from Mundola northward and on the east coast from Londo in Mozambique northward into Tanzanian waters.

Adult Size: 4 inches (9 cm).

Husbandry Requirements: A peaceful species that can be maintained in aquariums as small as 30 gallons (120 L). Provide sufficient hiding places and a thin layer of silica sand. Can be maintained with other peaceful species from the Haplochromis and Mbuna groups. Do not maintain with any other *Aulonocara* species, as hybridization is likely to occur.

Diet: Microinvertebrates hidden in the sand and on rocks. Offer a variety of commercially prepared aquarium foods. Supplement the diet with live baby brine shrimp and daphnia.

Breeding: Maintain several females to one or two males. Spawning will take place at regular intervals, and brooding females with join with the other females in a loose aggregation. Feed newly released juveniles live baby brine shrimp.

Name: *Aulonocara jacobfreibergi,* **Jakes, Malawi Butterfly, Mamalela Peacock**

Location and Natural Habitat: Found at Cape Maclear peninsula and along the entire west coast of the lake where suitable habitat of rocks and sand intermingle. Also found along the Tanzanian coastline.

Adult Size: To 4 inches (10 cm).

Husbandry Requirements: A peaceful species that can be maintained in aquariums as small as 30 gallons (120 L). Provide ample hiding places and a thin layer of silica sand. Can be maintained with other peaceful species from the Haplochromis and Mbuna groups. Do not maintain with any other *Aulonocara* species, as hybridization is likely to occur.

Diet: Microinvertebrates hidden in the sand and on rocks. Offer a variety of commercially prepared aquarium foods. Supplement the diet with live baby brine shrimp and daphnia.

Breeding: Maintain several females to one or two males. Spawning will take place at regular intervals, and brooding females with join with the other females in a loose aggregation. Feed newly released juveniles live baby brine shrimp.

Name: *Aulonocara* sp. **Maleri, Sunshine Peacock, Yellow Peacock**

Location and Natural Habitat: Found in the southeast arm of the lake primarily at Maleri, Nankoma, and Nakantenga Islands as well as at Chidunga Rocks. Inhabits the area where rocks and sand intermingle.

Adult Size: To 4 inches (10 cm).

Husbandry Requirements: A peaceful species that can be maintained in aquariums as small as 30 gallons (120 L). Provide ample hiding places and a thin layer of silica sand. Can be maintained with other peaceful species from the Haplochromis and Mbuna groups. Do not maintain with any other *Aulonocara* species, as hybridization is likely to occur.

Diet: Microinvertebrates hidden in the sand and on rocks. Offer a variety of commercially prepared aquarium foods. Supplement the diet with live baby brine shrimp and daphnia.

Aulonocara sp. Maleri was the first yellow Aulonocara species exported from the lake.

Breeding: Maintain several females to one or two males. Spawning will take place at regular intervals, and brooding females with join with the other females in a loose aggregation. Feed newly released juveniles live baby brine shrimp.

Name: *Buccochromis rhoadesii,* **Yellow Lepturus, Haplochromis lepturus**
Location and Natural Habitat: Found throughout the lake from shallow water to depths beyond 300 feet (90 m).

An often misidentified species from the lake is this **Buccochromis rhoadesii.**

In the wild, **Champsochromis caeruleus** *is an uncommon species that is usually seen alone.*

Adult Size: To 14 inches (35 cm).
Husbandry Requirements: A large, robust species that will need a large aquarium of at least 125 gallons (500 L). Provide a few large stones to form hiding places, while leaving much of the aquarium open for this species to cruise about. Best maintained in a community setup with large species of the Haplochromis group.
Diet: Small fish in the wild. Offer high-protein foods such as krill, feeder guppies, and commercially prepared frozen foods. Be careful not to overfeed.
Breeding: Maintain a single male with several females. After spawning, the female must be given a place to brood her eggs unmolested. Provide sufficient hiding places, or remove the female to another aquarium. Feed newly released juveniles live baby brine shrimp and finely crushed flake foods.

Name: *Champsochromis caeruleus,* **Haplochromis Thola, Haplochromis Trout**
Location and Natural Habitat: Found throughout the lake over a wide depth range.
Adult Size: To 15 inches (37 cm).
Husbandry Requirements: A large, agile species that needs a large aquarium for long-term successful maintenance. Aquarium should be no smaller than 150 gallons (600 L) with only a few smooth stones to serve as hiding places, and plenty of open water.
Diet: Small fish in the wild. Offer high-protein foods such as krill, feeder guppies, and commercially prepared frozen foods. Be careful not to overfeed.
Breeding: Maintain a single male with several females. After spawning, the female must be given a place to brood her eggs unmolested.

Pictured is a subadult male **Champsochromis spilorynchus.**

Pictured is a **Chilotilapia rhoadesii** *in full spawning colors.*

Provide sufficient hiding places for the female to retreat to, or remove the female to another aquarium. Feed newly released juveniles live baby brine shrimp and finely crushed flake foods.

Name: *Champsochromis spilorynchus*
Location and Natural Habitat: Found throughout the lake over a wide depth range.
Adult Size: To 13 inches (32.5 cm).
Husbandry Requirements: A large, agile species that needs a large aquarium if it is to be maintained properly. Aquarium should be no smaller than 150 gallons (600 L) with only a few smooth stones and plenty of open space.
Diet: Small fish in the wild. Young individuals occasionally seen near the nest of the catfish, *Bagrus meridionalis*, opportunistically dining on their babies. Offer high-protein foods such as krill, feeder guppies, and commercially prepared frozen foods. Be careful not to overfeed.
Breeding: Maintain a single male with several females. After spawning, the female must be given a place to brood her eggs unmolested.

Provide sufficient hiding places, or remove the female to another aquarium. Feed newly released juveniles live baby brine shrimp and finely crushed flake foods.

Name: *Chilotilapia rhoadesii*
Location and Natural Habitat: Found throughout the lake over a wide depth range.
Adult Size: To 12 inches (30 cm).
Husbandry Requirements: A large, moderately peaceful species. Large individuals will need an aquarium of at least 100 gallons (400 L). Can be maintained in a community aquarium with other mild-mannered species of the Haplochromis group. Can also be kept with nonaggressive species of the Mbuna group. Provide plenty of open space with very little rocks.
Diet: Snails in the wild. Offer high-protein foods such as fresh shrimp, chopped scallops, or krill.
Breeding: Best maintained in groups of at least 12. The male will select an area of the aquarium to spawn and coax any receptive female to its nest. After spawning, the brooding

Most **Copadichromis azureus** *that are collected come from Mbenji Island.*

Several color variants of **Copadichromis borleyi** *are known throughout the lake. This male is from Mbenji Island.*

female may join with the other females for the duration of the brooding period. Feed juveniles live baby brine shrimp and finely crushed flake foods.

Name: *Copadichromis azureus,* **Haplochromis Chrysonotus**

Location and Natural Habitat: Found primarily at Mbenji Island in areas where rocks and sand meet.

Adult Size: To 6 inches (15 cm).

Husbandry Requirements: Best maintained in a large group of at least 15 individuals. Provide a tall aquarium with plenty of swimming space for nonspawning males and females, as well as a shallow layer of silica sand and a few smooth stones. Use no smaller than a 75-gallon (300 L) aquarium.

Diet: Plankton in the wild. Offer a variety of commercially prepared aquarium foods. Supplement the diet with live baby brine shrimp and daphnia.

Breeding: Male digs a pit in the sand next to the rocks and coaxes any receptive female to spawn. After spawning, the brooding female

joins with the other females to brood her eggs. It is not uncommon for the male to spawn with several females within a couple of days. Feed juveniles live baby brine shrimp.

Name: *Copadichromis borleyi,* **Haplochromis quadrimaculatus, Red Fin Kadango**

Location and Natural Habitat: Found throughout the lake wherever large rocks are present.

Adult Size: To 5 inches (12.5 cm).

Husbandry Requirements: Best maintained in groups of at least 15 individuals. Provide a tall aquarium with plenty of swimming space for nonspawning males and females, as well as a shallow layer of silica sand and a few large stones. Aquarium should be no smaller than 75 gallons (300 L).

Diet: Plankton in the wild. Offer a variety of commercially prepared aquarium foods. Supplement the diet with live baby brine shrimp and daphnia.

Breeding: Sexually active males will spawn on the large stones. After spawning, the brooding female joins with the other females to brood her eggs. It is not uncommon for the male to spawn with several females within a couple of days. Feed juveniles live baby brine shrimp.

Name: *Copadichromis trewavasae*, **Mloto Likoma, Haplochromis Ivoryhead**
Location and Natural Habitat: Found at Likoma and Chizumulu Islands as well as along the east coast in Tanzanian waters from Manda to Lupingu.
Adult Size: To 6 inches (15 cm).
Husbandry Requirements: Best maintained in groups at least 15 individuals. Provide a tall aquarium with plenty of swimming space for nonspawning males and females, as well as a shallow layer of silica sand and a few smooth stones. Use no smaller than a 75-gallon (300 L) aquarium.
Diet: Plankton in the wild. Offer a variety of commercially prepared aquarium foods. Supplement the diet with live baby brine shrimp and daphnia.
Breeding: Male digs a pit in the sand next to the rocks and coaxes any receptive female to spawn. After spawning, the brooding female joins with other females to brood her clutch. It is not uncommon for the male to spawn with several females within a couple of days. Feed juveniles live baby brine shrimp.

Name: *Copadichromis verduyni*, **Eastern Borleyi**
Location and Natural Habitat: Found only on the east coast of Malawi from Makanjila Point to Masinje. Inhabits the area where rocks and sand intermingle.
Adult Size: To 5 inches (12.5 cm).
Husbandry Requirements: Maintain in a group setup of at least ten individuals. Provide

a thin layer of silica sand and several smooth stones with plenty of open space above. Aquarium should be no smaller than 50 gallons (200 L).
Diet: Plankton in the wild. Offer a variety of commercially prepared aquarium foods. Supplement the diet with live baby brine shrimp and daphnia.
Breeding: Males can harass females, so provide enough refuge for brooding females to retreat to after spawning. Brooding females will join with the other females in the upper

Pictured is a male **Copadichromis trewavasae** *from Lupingu, Tanzania.*

Pictured is a male **Copadichromis verduyni** *from Masinje, Malawi.*

Pictured is a **Copadichromis virginalis** *from the east coast at Masinje, Malawi.*

The bulging forehead is characteristic of **Crytocara moorii.**

water column to brood their eggs. Feed juveniles live baby brine shrimp.

Name: *Copadichromis virginalis*, **Firecrest Mloto**

Location and Natural Habitat: Found on the east coast in Malawi from Makanjila Point to at least Gome. Probably occurs within Mozambique waters. Normally inhabits depths of 100 to 150 feet (30–45 m).

Adult Size: To 5 inches (12.5 cm).

Husbandry Requirements: Since it is found in deep water, an aquarium with no lighting above is recommended. The natural colors of this species will come out more in an aquarium illuminated with ambient light. Maintain a shallow layer of silica sand and a few large, smooth stones. Several males and females can be maintained together in an aquarium as small as 50 gallons (200 L).

Diet: Plankton in the wild. Offer a variety of commercially prepared aquarium foods. Supplement the diet with live baby brine shrimp and daphnia.

Breeding: The male digs a pit in the sand next to the rocks and coaxes any receptive female to spawn. After spawning, the brooding female joins with the other females to brood her eggs. It is not uncommon for the male to spawn with several females within a couple of days. Feed juveniles live baby brine shrimp.

Name: *Crytocara moorii*, **Blue Dolphin**

Location and Natural Habitat: Found throughout the lake wherever sandy areas are present. Usually seen in shallow water.

Adult Size: To 8 inches (20 cm).

Husbandry Requirements: A peaceful species. Best maintained in groups of six, or in a community aquarium with other species of the Haplochromis group. Can also be maintained with species of the Mbuna group. Aquarium should be no smaller than 75 gallons (300 L). The aquarium interior should consist of a thin layer of silica sand and a few large, smooth stones.

Diet: Invertebrates hidden in the sand that have been stirred up by sand-sifting species of the genus *Taeniolethrinops*. Offer a variety of commercially prepared aquarium foods such as flakes, pellets, krill, ocean plankton, and frozen foods.

Breeding: Males can be distinguished from females by the larger hump on the forehead. The dominant male will spawn with any receptive female present. The brooding female can be left with the male without being overly harassed. Feed newly released juveniles live baby brine shrimp and finely crushed flake foods.

Name: *Dimidiochromis compressiceps*
Location and Natural Habitat: Found throughout the lake, primarily in shallow areas with reed beds.
Adult Size: To 10 inches (25 cm).
Husbandry Requirements: Because of its relatively large size and aggressive nature, it will require an aquarium of at least 100 gallons (400 L). Provide open sandy areas as well as several rocks piled up to form caves and passageways.
Diet: Juvenile fish in shallow reed beds in the wild. Offer high-protein foods such as krill, feeder guppies, and commercially prepared frozen foods.

Breeding: The male becomes quite aggressive during periods of sexual activity. Only receptive females are permitted into the male's territory to spawn. Afterwards, the brooding female will find a secluded place to brood her eggs unmolested. You may need to remove the female to another aquarium if sufficient hiding places are not available. Feed newly released juveniles live baby brine shrimp.

Name: *Dimidiochromis strigatus*, **Sunset Haplochromis**
Location and Natural Habitat: Found throughout the lake in shallow water wherever there are aquatic plants.
Adult Size: To 10 inches (25 cm).
Husbandry Requirements: Best maintained in a community aquarium with other species of the Haplochromis group in an aquarium of at least 100 gallons (400 L). Provide open sandy areas as well as several rocks piled up to form caves and passageways.
Diet: Juvenile fishes in the wild. Offer high-protein foods such as krill, feeder guppies, and commercially prepared frozen foods.

Dimidiochromis compressiceps is perhaps the most laterally compressed Malawi cichlid.

Pictured is a male **Dimidiochromis strigatus.**

Breeding: The male may construct a nest in the sand and coax any receptive female to spawn. Afterwards, the brooding female will need to find a secluded place to brood her eggs unmolested. You may need to remove the female to another aquarium if sufficient hiding places are not present. Feed newly released juveniles live baby brine shrimp.

Name: *Eclectochromis milomo,*
Haplochromis VC-10
Location and Natural Habitat: Found throughout the lake. Inhabits deep water ranging from 50 to 150 feet (15–45 m) where it is commonly found over rocky areas.
Adult Size: To 10 inches (25 cm).
Husbandry Requirements: A relatively large, robust species that requires an aquarium that is at least 100 gallons (400 L). Provide a sufficient amount of rocks piled up to form caves and passageways, as well as open space. Do not maintain with highly aggressive species of the Mbuna group.
Diet: Invertebrates hidden in the cracks of rocks. Offer a varied diet of commercially prepared aquarium foods such as flakes, pellets,

ocean plankton, and frozen foods. Be careful not to overfeed.
Breeding: The dominant male will establish a territory among the rocks as its spawning site. The brooding female should be provided with a secluded place to brood her eggs. Feed newly released juveniles live baby brine shrimp.

Name: *Eclectochromis* sp. **Mbenji Thick Lips, Labrosus Mbenji**
Location and Natural Habitat: Found only at Mbenji Island. Commonly inhabits the area where the sand and rocks intermingle. The visibility of the water is often limited by the amount of sediments normally encountered around this island.
Adult Size: To 10 inches (25 cm).
Husbandry Requirements: A large, active species that will need an aquarium of at least 150 gallons (600 L). Provide an even amount of rocks piled up to form caves and passageways and a fine layer of silica sand. An ideal candidate for a Malawi cichlid community aquarium.
Diet: Invertebrates and small fishes hidden in the cracks of rocks. Offer a varied diet of commercially prepared aquarium foods such as

Pictured is a female **Eclectochromis milomo** *from Masinje.*

Eclectochromis *sp. Thick Lip Mbenji is from Mbenji Island.*

A sexually active male Exochochromis anagenys *collected from the Tanzanian coastline.*

Lethrinops cf. lethrinus *is one of the more peaceful species of the Haplochromis group.*

fresh shrimp, flakes, pellets, ocean plankton, and frozen foods. Be careful not to overfeed.

Breeding: The male will stake out a territory among the rocks where spawning will take place. Afterwards, the brooding female will join with the other females in the open to brood her eggs to full term. Feed newly released juveniles live baby brine shrimp.

Name: *Exochochromis anagenys*

Location and Natural Habitat: Found throughout the lake in all kinds of habitat.

Adult Size: To 12 inches (30 cm).

Husbandry Requirements: The large size of this species dictates that it be housed in an aquarium no smaller than 150 gallons (600 L). Best maintained in a community arrangement with similar-sized Malawi cichlids of the Haplochromis group. Provide a few large, smooth stones and plenty of open space.

Diet: Small fishes in the wild. Offer high-protein foods such as krill, feeder guppies, and commercially prepared frozen foods.

Breeding: The male's coloration intensifies during periods of sexual activity. Only receptive

females are permitted into the male's territory to spawn. Afterwards, the brooding female will find a secluded place to brood her eggs. You may need to remove the female to another aquarium if sufficient hiding places are not present. Feed newly released juveniles live baby brine shrimp.

Name: *Lethrinops cf. lethrinus*

Location and Natural Habitat: Found throughout the lake over sandy habitats.

Adult Size: To 5 inches (12.5 cm).

Husbandry Requirements: A peaceful species that should be maintained in an aquarium with very few rocks. Provide a thin layer of silica sand and a couple of smooth stones to help demarcate territories. This species can be adequately housed in aquariums as small as 40 gallons (160 L).

Diet: Small crustaceans hidden in the sand. Offer a varied diet, with an emphasis on small live foods such as baby brine shrimp and daphnia.

Breeding: If given enough sand, the male will construct a sand nest. Any receptive female will enter the nest for the spawning. Afterwards, the female will leave the male's nest and incubate her eggs with the other females. Feed newly released juveniles live baby brine shrimp.

Name: *Lethrinops* sp. **Nyassae**

Location and Natural Habitat: Found throughout the lake wherever there is a mixture of sand and rocks. Usually found at a depth of 50 to 100 feet (45–90 m).

Adult Size: To 4½ inches (11 cm).

Husbandry Requirements: A peaceful species that should be maintained in an aquarium with very few rocks. Provide a thin layer of silica sand and a couple of large, smooth stones to help demarcate territories. Can be adequately housed in aquariums as small as 40 gallons (160 L).

Diet: Small crustaceans hidden in the sand. Offer a varied diet, with an emphasis on small live foods such as live baby brine shrimp and daphnia.

Breeding: The male will construct a sand nest next to a rock and attempt to entice any nearby female to spawn. If no rocks are present, the male may randomly construct a shal-

low pit. After spawning, the female will leave the male's nest and incubate her eggs with the other females. Feed newly released juveniles live baby brine shrimp.

Name: *Lichnochromis acuticeps,* **Malawi Gar**

Location and Natural Habitat: Found throughout the lake over shallow, rocky areas.

Adult Size: To 12 inches (30 cm).

Husbandry Requirements: A mild-mannered, shy species. Best to maintain at least six together in a community aquarium of other species of the Haplochromis group. Provide plenty of rocks piled up to form caves and passageways. Use no smaller than a 75-gallon (300 L) aquarium.

Diet: Small fishes in the wild. Offer high-protein foods such as krill, feeder guppies, and commercially prepared frozen foods.

Breeding: Spawning will take place anywhere in the aquarium. Brooding females are particularly shy and will invariably retire to a hidden area of the aquarium while brooding their eggs. Feed juveniles live baby brine shrimp.

Lethrinops sp. Nyassae should be provided with silica sand to bring out its natural sand-sifting behavior.

Lichnochromis acuticeps appears to be a peaceful, timid species in captivity.

Name: *Mylochromis gracilis*

Location and Natural Habitat: Found mainly in the southern half of the lake in sandy habitats.

Adult Size: To 10 inches (25 cm).

Husbandry Requirements: Best maintained in groups of eight. A nervous species that is best kept in a dimly lit aquarium. The aquarium should be no smaller than 75 gallons (300 L). Provide a combination of rocks and a shallow layer of silica sand.

Diet: Fishes in the wild. Offer high-protein foods such as krill, feeder guppies, and commercially prepared frozen foods.

Breeding: The male will construct a nest in the sand. The female will spawn within the male's nest, and after spawning leave to incubate her eggs in a quiet place. Feed newly released juveniles live baby brine shrimp.

Name: *Mylochromis* sp. **Lateristriga Makanjila, Haplochromis Mola**

Location and Natural Habitat: Found on the east coast of the lake from Makanjila Point northward to Gome. Inhabits the area where there is an even mixture of rocks and sand.

Mylochromis gracilis is a rarely encountered cichlid in the lake.

Adult Size: To 6 inches (15 cm).

Husbandry Requirements: A slow-growing, delicate species. Provide plenty of rocks piled up to form caves and passageways. Will die if water quality is not kept up to meticulous standards. Can be maintained with other Malawi cichlids from the Mbuna group that are not too aggressive. Use no smaller than a 75-gallon (300 L) aquarium.

Diet: Small crustaceans hidden in the sand. Offer a varied diet, with an emphasis on small live foods such as brine shrimp, mosquito larvae, and daphnia.

Breeding: The male will construct a sand nest next to a rock and entice any nearby female to spawn. After spawning, the female will leave the male's nest and incubate her eggs in seclusion. Feed newly released juveniles live baby brine shrimp.

Name: *Nimbochromis fuscotaeniatus*

Location and Natural Habitat: Found in the southern third of the lake. Normally observed in areas where sand and rocks intermingle in shallow water.

Adult Size: To 10 inches (25 cm).

Mylochromis sp. Lateristriga Makanjila from Makanjila Point grows slowly in captivity.

Nimbochromis fuscotaeniatus *is piscivorous by nature.*

Husbandry Requirements: A robust, hardy, and active species that will require an aquarium of at least 150 gallons (600 L). Provide plenty of rocks piled up to form caves and passageways as well as open spaces. Can easily be maintained in a community aquarium with other aggressive species from the Haplochromis or Mbuna groups.

Diet: Small fishes in the wild. Offer high-protein foods such as krill, feeder guppies, fresh shrimp, and commercially prepared frozen foods.

Breeding: The male becomes particularly aggressive during periods of sexual activity. Provide hiding places for the brooding female to retreat to after spawning since the male may be overly aggressive. May be advisable to remove the female to a separate aquarium to brood her eggs. Feed juveniles live baby brine shrimp and finely crushed flake foods.

Name: *Nimbochromis linni,* **Elephant Nose Polystigma**

Location and Natural Habitat: Found throughout the lake over a wide variety of habitats.

Adult Size: To 14 inches (35 cm).

Husbandry Requirements: A large, delicate species that must have scrupulously clean water. Frequent large-scale water changes are crucial if this cichlid is to be maintained successfully. Can be maintained in a community setup with similar-sized species of the Haplochromis group. The aquarium should be no smaller than 100 gallons (400 L). Do not maintain with other *Nimbochromis* species as hybridization may occur.

Diet: Fishes in the wild. Offer high-protein foods such as krill, feeder guppies, fresh shrimp and commercially prepared frozen foods. Be careful not to overfeed.

Breeding: The male will stake out a large portion of the aquarium as its spawning site. After spawning, the female will need to find a secluded place to brood her eggs. She may need to be removed to a quieter aquarium if the male is too aggressive. Feed newly released juveniles live baby brine shrimp and finely crushed flake foods.

Nimbochromis linni *is an ambush predator.*

Name: *Nimbochromis livingstonii*
Location and Natural Habitat: Found throughout the lake over areas where sand and rocks intermingle.
Adult Size: To 10 inches (25 cm).
Husbandry Requirements: A robust species that will need an aquarium of at least 100 gallons (400). Provide an even mixture of rocks piled up to form caves, as well as a thin layer of silica sand. Do not maintain with other *Nimbochromis* species as hybridization may occur.
Diet: Fishes in the wild. Offer high-protein foods such as krill, feeder guppies, fresh shrimp, and commercially prepared frozen foods.
Breeding: The spawning male loses the mottled brown-and-white pattern and develops a bluish cast. After spawning, the female will find a secluded area to brood her eggs. She may need to be removed to a quieter aquarium if she cannot evade the male's heightened aggression. Feed newly released juveniles live baby brine shrimp and finely crushed flake foods.

Name: *Nimbochromis polystigma*
Location and Natural Habitat: Found throughout the lake over areas where the sand and rocks intermingle.
Adult Size: To 10 inches (25 cm).
Husbandry Requirements: A robust species that will need an aquarium of at least 100 gallons (400). Provide an even mixture of rocks piled up to form caves as well as a thin layer of silica sand. Do not maintain with other *Nimbochromis* species as hybridization may occur.
Diet: Fishes in the wild. Offer high-protein foods such as krill, feeder guppies, fresh shrimp, and commercially prepared frozen foods. Be careful not to overfeed.

Pictured is a brooding female **Nimbochromis livingstonii** *from Likoma Island.*

Breeding: The spawning male loses the freckled brown and white pattern and develops a dark blue color. After spawning, the female will find a secluded area to brood her eggs. Feed newly released juveniles live baby brine shrimp and finely crushed flake foods.

Name: *Nimbochromis venustus*
Location and Natural Habitat: Found throughout the lake wherever sandy regions are present.
Adult Size: To 10 inches (25 cm).

Nimbochromis polystigma *occasionally feigns death to attract juvenile cichlids to consume.*

The species of the genus **Nimbochromis** *least likely to be encountered in the wild is* **N. venustus.**

A male Otopharynx lithobates *from Zimbawe Rock in full spawning coloration is shown here.*

Husbandry Requirements: A sand-dwelling species that should be maintained in a large aquarium—at least 100 gallons (400 L)—with little or no rocks present. Can be maintained with other Malawi cichlids too large to be eaten.

Diet: Fishes in the wild. Offer high-protein foods such as krill, feeder guppies, fresh shrimp, and commercially prepared frozen foods. Be careful not to overfeed.

Breeding: Spawning will take place any-where in the aquarium. Provide a single male with several females to spread out the male's aggressive tendencies. Feed newly released juveniles live baby brine shrimp and finely crushed flake food.

Name: *Otopharynx lithobates,* **Yellow Blaze Aristochromis, Red Top Aristochromis**
Location and Natural Habitat: Found at Cape Maclear peninsula and the nearby islands. Each location sports a distinctly colored dorsal fin.
Adult Size: To 6 inches (15 cm).
Husbandry Requirements: A cave dweller that should be provided with large rocks piled up to form spacious caves. A mild-mannered species that can be maintained with other peaceful Malawi cichlids. Aquarium should be at least 75 gallons (300 L).
Diet: Omnivorous. Picks at anything edible on the surface of large rocks in its natural habitat. Offer a variety of commercially pre-pared aquarium foods such as flakes, pellets, krill, ocean plankton, and frozen foods.
Breeding: The sexually active male will entice any nearby female to spawn within its cave. Afterwards, the brooding female will find a secluded place to brood her eggs. Due to the mild nature of this species, the female can remain with the male in the same aquarium without being overly harassed. Feed newly released juveniles live baby brine shrimp.

Name: *Otopharynx walteri*
Location and Natural Habitat: Found at Nakantenga Island at depths greater than 40 feet (12 m). Inhabits the dark recesses of the rocky areas.

Otopharynx walteri is found only at Nakantenga Island.

Otopharynx sp. Blue Otter is a commanding species that often swims with its fins erect.

Adult Size: To 6 inches (15 cm).

Husbandry Requirements: A shy, peaceful species that is best maintained in an aquarium to itself. If kept in a community setup, the other inhabitants must not dominate. Provide large rocks piled up to form caves. Aquarium should be at least 75 gallons (300 L).

Diet: Small fishes and invertebrates in the wild. Offer-high protein foods such as krill, feeder guppies, fresh shrimp, and commercially prepared frozen foods. Be careful not to over-feed.

Breeding: The dominant male will spawn with any receptive female in the privacy of his cave. Brooding females will find a place to brood their eggs in seclusion. Feed newly released juveniles live baby brine shrimp.

Name: *Otopharynx* sp. **Blue Otter, Domwe Reef Granderus**

Location and Natural Habitat: Found at Cape Maclear National Park and southward down the Nankhumba Peninsula. Inhabits the area where large rocks meet the sand.

Adult Size: To 5 inches (12.5 cm).

Husbandry Requirements: A relatively peaceful species that is best housed in a community aquarium with other mild-mannered Malawi cichlids. Provide large, smooth stones and a thin layer of silica sand. Aquarium should be at least 50 gallons (200 L).

Diet: Invertebrates in the sand and rocks in the wild. Offer a variety of commercially prepared foods such as flakes, pellets, freeze-dried ocean plankton, and various frozen foods.

Breeding: The dominant male will establish his spawning site on the top of a large, flat surface. After spawning, the brooding female will congregate with the other females. Feed juveniles live baby brine shrimp.

Name: "*Otopharynx*" sp. **Silver Torpedo**

Location and Natural Habitat: Found in the southern half of the lake over sandy areas. A very uncommon species.

Adult Size: To 7 inches (17.5 cm).

Husbandry Requirements: A peaceful species that should not be maintained with aggressive Malawi cichlids of either the Haplochromis or Mbuna group. Provide a few smooth stones and a large open, sandy bottom with a thin layer of silica sand. Best kept by itself in groups no smaller than 12. The aquarium should be at least 75 gallons (300 L).

Diet: Invertebrates hidden in the sand. Offer a variety of commercially prepared foods such as flakes, pellets, freeze-dried ocean plankton, and various frozen foods.

Breeding: The dominant male may dig a shallow pit in the sand and spawn with any receptive female. After spawning, the brooding females will join with the other females to incubate their eggs to full term. Feed newly released juveniles live baby brine shrimp.

Name: *Placidochromis electra*, **Deep Water Hap**

Location and Natural Habitat: Found at Likoma Island and along the entire Mozambique coastline down into Malawi as far south as Fort Maguire. Inhabits sandy areas.

Adult Size: To 6 inches (15 cm).

Husbandry Requirements: An ideal beginner's Malawi cichlid. Maintain in groups of six in a community aquarium of Malawi cichlids from the Haplochromis group. The aquarium should have a fine layer of silica sand with a few smooth stones scattered about. Provide plenty of swimming space. Do not mix this species with *P. phenochilus*, as hybridization may occur. Aquarium should be at least 50 gallons (200 L).

Diet: Invertebrates hidden in the sand that have been stirred up by sand-sifting cichlids. Offer a varied diet of flakes, frozen foods, and pellets.

Breeding: Spawning will take place anywhere in the aquarium, although the male may stake out a particular area of the aquarium as his territory and preferred spawning site. Brooding females can be left with the male as long as there are other fishes in the aquarium to distract the male's sexually aggressive tendencies. Feed newly released juveniles live baby brine shrimp and finely crushed flake foods.

Name: *Placidochromis phenochilus*

Location and Natural Habitat: Found in the northern part of the lake. Typically inhabits the sandy areas at depths greater than 50 feet (15 m). An exceptionally rare species.

"Otopharynx" sp. Silver Torpedo is a very uncommon species in the lake.

The Deep Water Hap, Placidochromis electra, is an ideal beginner's cichlid.

Pictured is a captive-reared male **Placido-chromis phenochilus** *whose parents originated from Lupingu, Tanzania.*

Placidochromis sp. *Johnstoni Solo is normally seen alone in the wild.*

Adult Size: To 6 inches (15 cm).

Husbandry Requirements: A mild-mannered, easy-to-maintain species. Best kept in groups of ten. Provide a fine layer of silica sand, with plenty of open space and a few smooth stones. Do not mix this species with *P. electra*, as hybridization may occur. Aquarium should be at least 50 gallons (200 L).

Diet: Invertebrates in the sand in the wild. Offer a varied diet consisting of flakes, pellets, freeze-dried ocean plankton, and frozen foods.

Breeding: Spawning takes place anywhere in the aquarium. Males do not particularly harass females, so brooding females can remain with the dominant male. Brooding females will tend to congregate with the other females. Feed juveniles live baby brine shrimp.

Name: *Placidochromis* sp. **Johnstoni Solo, Haplochromis Thick Bars**

Location and Natural Habitat: Found throughout the lake. An uncommon species that is normally seen over rocky areas in very clear water.

Adult Size: To 5 inches (12.5 cm).

Husbandry Requirements: A delicate species that will not tolerate improper water quality. A peaceful, nonterritorial species that can be maintained in aquariums as small as 50 gallons (200 L). Best maintained by itself, or with other peaceful species. Be careful not to overfeed.

Diet: Invertebrates hidden in the rocks. Offer a varied diet consisting of flakes, pellets, freeze-dried ocean plankton, and frozen foods.

Breeding: Should be the only species in the aquarium if spawning is to take place, as the dominant male is easily intimidated by more aggressive species. Spawning takes place anywhere in the aquarium, and the brooding female will retire to a quiet place to incubate her eggs. Feed juveniles live baby brine shrimp.

Name: *Protomelas annectens*

Location and Natural Habitat: Found throughout the lake over sandy areas in shallow water.

Adult Size: To 7 inches (17.5 cm).

Husbandry Requirements: A good beginner's species to start with. Can be maintained with other Malawi cichlids of either the

Protomelas annectens *can be maintained with other peaceful cichlids from the Mbuna group.*

The Fire Blue Hap was scientifically described in 1993 as Protomelas dejunctus.

Haplochromis or Mbuna group. Provide a shallow layer of silica sand and rock piled up to form caves and passageways. The aquarium should be at least 75 gallons (300 L).

Diet: Invertebrates hidden in the sand that have been stirred up by sand-sifting species of the genus *Taeniolethrinops.* Offer a varied diet consisting of flakes, pellets, freeze-dried ocean plankton, and frozen foods.

Breeding: Spawning will take place anywhere in the aquarium. Brooding females are usually ignored and can be left together with the male. Feed newly released juveniles live baby brine shrimp and finely crushed flake foods.

Name: *Protomelas dejunctus,* **Fire Blue Haplochromis**

Location and Natural Habitat: Found at Chinyamwezi and Chinyankwazi Islands in the southeast arm of the lake. Inhabits rocky areas at a depth of approximately 20 feet (6 m).

Adult Size: To 6 inches (15 cm).

Husbandry Requirements: Can be maintained in a community aquarium with species of the Haplochromis group. Provide large rocks to form caves and passageways. The aquarium should be at least 75 gallons (300 L).

Diet: Invertebrates and plankton in the wild. Offer a varied diet consisting of flakes, pellets, freeze-dried ocean plankton, and frozen foods.

Breeding: Spawning usually takes place on top of a rock. The brooding female will join with the other females to brood her eggs to full term. Feed juveniles live baby brine shrimp.

Name: *Protomelas marginatus,* **Blue Fenestratus**

Location and Natural Habitat: Found throughout the lake in shallow, heavily silted water. Inhabits sandy areas wherever plants are present.

Adult Size: To 5 inches (12.5 cm).

Husbandry Requirements: An easy species to maintain provided the water quality is kept to meticulous standards. Provide a thin layer of silica sand and several large smooth stones. Use no smaller than a 75-gallon (300 L) aquarium.

Diet: Algae, plants, invertebrates, and sponges in the wild. Offer a varied diet consisting of flakes, pellets, freeze-dried ocean plankton, and frozen foods.

Breeding: Spawning will take place anywhere in the aquarium. Brooding females are usually ignored and can be left together with the male. Feed newly released juveniles live baby brine shrimp and finely crushed flake foods.

Name: *Protomelas fenestratus,* **Tiger Steveni, Steveni Eastern, Haplochromis Steveni**
Location and Natural Habitat: Found throughout the lake in areas where the rocks and sand intermingle at depths no greater than 40 feet (13 m).
Adult Size: To 6 inches (15 cm).
Husbandry Requirements: Best maintained in groups of eight. Arrange plenty of rocks piled up to form caves and passageways, while providing ample swimming space above the rocks. Avoid maintaining with highly aggressive species from the Mbuna group. Use no smaller than a 75-gallon (300 L) aquarium.
Diet: Feeds on invertebrates in the sand by blowing a jet of water to dislodge them from hiding. Offer a varied diet consisting of flakes, pellets, freeze-dried ocean plankton, and frozen foods.
Breeding: The dominant male will stake out a territory and entice any receptive female to spawn. After spawning, the female should be provided with a secluded area to hide in so that she can brood her eggs without being overly harassed by the male. Feed newly released juveniles live baby brine shrimp.

Name: *Protomelas* sp. **Spilonotus Tanzania**
Location and Natural Habitat: Found along the Tanzanian coastline from Mbamba Bay to Ikombe. Inhabits shallow water next to large boulders.

Pictured is a male **Protomelas marginatus** *in spawning coloration.*

A male **Protomelas fenestratus** *from Chizumulu Island.*

Adult Size: To 7 inches (17.5 cm).
Husbandry Requirements: A relatively delicate, slow-growing species that will need an aquarium all to itself; otherwise, it should be the dominant species in the aquarium. Provide plenty of large rocks and a lot of open space above. House this species in a tall aquarium of at least 100 gallons (400 L).
Diet: Plankton in the wild. Offer a varied diet of commercially prepared aquarium foods.

Supplement the diet with live baby brine shrimp and daphnia. Be careful not to overfeed.

Breeding: Males will coax any receptive female to their territory to spawn. If several

Protomelas sp. Spilonotus Tanzania is a large, delicate species that should be housed in a large aquarium with other non-aggressive tankmates. Pictured is a wild male collected from Lundo Island, Tanzania.

Protomelas sp. Steveni Taiwan can quickly lose much of its natural coloration in captivity through successive inbreeding. Make every effort not to spawn brother to sister, and instead look for wild- or first-generation offspring to mix with existing stocks. Pictured is a spawning male from Taiwan Reef.

females are housed with the male, the brooding female will join with the other females for security while brooding her eggs. Feed newly released juveniles live baby brine shrimp.

Name: *Protomelas* sp. **Steveni Taiwan**
Location and Natural Habitat: Found at Taiwan Reed just north of Chizumulu Island as well as at Mbamba Bay, Mbamba Bay (Ngkuyo) Island, and Higga Reef in Tanzania. Inhabits the top of Taiwan Reef to a depth of 45 feet (14 m) but inhabits shallower waters on the mainland. Can be found only over rocky areas in very clear water.

Adult Size: To 6 inches (15 cm).

Husbandry Requirements: A delicate species that must have very clean water. Frequent large-scale water changes are vital if this cichlid is to be maintained successfully. Can be maintained in a community setup with similar-sized species of the Haplochromis group if it is the dominant species. Aquarium should be no smaller than 75 gallons (300 L) with several large, smooth stones.

Diet: Anything edible on the surface of large boulders. Offer a varied diet consisting of flakes, pellets, freeze-dried ocean plankton, and frozen foods.

Breeding: The dominant male will aggressively defend his spawning site on the top of a large rock and entice any receptive female to spawn. After spawning, the brooding female may stay hidden among the rocks. Feed juveniles live baby brine shrimp.

Name: *Protomelas cf. taeniolatus,* **Red Empress**
Location and Natural Habitat: Found only at Namalenje Island in Senga Bay, Malawi.

Inhabits the silt-filled rocks of this island at the zone where the sand and rocks meet. The depth of the water is shallow with a maximum depth of 20 feet (6 m).

Adult Size: To 5 inches (12.5 cm).

Husbandry Requirements: An ideal beginner's species. The aquarium should be no smaller than 50 gallons (200 L) with plenty of rocks piled up to form caves and passageways. Do not maintain with highly aggressive species of the Mbuna group.

Diet: Invertebrates from the rocks and sand. Offer a varied diet consisting of flakes, pellets, freeze-dried ocean plankton, and frozen foods.

Breeding: Best spawned in a group with one or two males and several females. Spawning commences when females become ripe with eggs. Brooding females hold their own and are apparently not bothered by the aggressiveness of the males. Feed juveniles live baby brine shrimp and finely crushed flake foods.

Name: *Rhamphochromis cf. macrophthalmus,* **Malawi Barracuda**

Location and Natural Habitat: Found throughout the lake in open, shallow water near shore.

Adult Size: To 9 inches (22 cm).

Husbandry Requirements: A peaceful, easy species to maintain in spite of its piscivorous appearance and tendencies in the wild. Best maintained with other species of the Haplochromis group that are not too aggressive. Aquarium should be no smaller than 100 gallons (400 L).

Diet: Small fishes in the wild. Will accept a wide variety of commercially prepared foods. Offer foods high in protein.

The Red Empress, **Protomelas cf. taeniolatus,** *hails from Namalenje Island. Pictured is a captive-reared male.*

The Malawi Barracuda, **Rhamphochromis cf. macrophthalmus,** *is the only species of the genus* **Rhamphochromis** *to have become established in aquariums. In spite of its predatory appearance and dietary preference for small fish, captive specimens will accept a variety of commercially prepared aquarium foods.*

Breeding: Spawns readily in captivity. The dominant male will spawn over a shallow depression in the sand or in midwater. Brooding females will join with the other females to brood their eggs. Feed juveniles live baby brine shrimp and finely crushed flake foods.

The Electric Blue, Sciaenochromis fryeri, has long been a popular aquarium fish due to its brilliant coloration. Throughout its history in the aquarium hobby, it had been repeatedly misidentified, but was officially described in 1993 by Ad Konings.

Stigmatochromis modestus is a cryptic species that requires ample hiding places in which to lurk about and feel secure.

Name: *Sciaenochromis fryeri,* **Electric Blue Hap, Haplochromis ahli**

Location and Natural Habitat: Found throughout the lake over a variety of habitats. Usually found within the vicinity of rocks.

Adult Size: To 6 inches (15 cm).

Husbandry Requirements: An ideal beginner's species. Provide the aquarium with a fine layer of silica sand and several rocks piled up to form caves and passageways. Aquarium should be at least 75 gallons (300 L).

Diet: Small fishes in the wild. Will accept a wide variety of commercially prepared foods such as fresh shrimp, flakes, pellets, and ocean plankton. Supplement the diet with live feeder guppies.

Breeding: The dominant male will spawn with any and all receptive females. Brooding females will find a secluded area to incubate their eggs. Feed newly released juveniles live baby brine shrimp.

Name: *Stigmatochromis modestus*

Location and Natural Habitat: Found throughout the lake wherever rocks are present. A very cryptic species, not likely to be seen out in the open.

Adult Size: To 7 inches (17.5 cm).

Husbandry Requirements: A shy species that should be provided with plenty of rocks piled up to form caves and passageways. Can be maintained with other Malawi cichlids too large to be swallowed. Use no smaller than a 75-gallon (300 L) aquarium.

Diet: Small fishes in the wild. Offer a high-protein diet of fresh shrimp, freeze-dried krill, guppies, and commercially prepared frozen foods.

Breeding: Spawning will take place in seclusion among the rocks. Brooding females will also stay hidden to brood their eggs to full term. Feed newly released juveniles live baby brine shrimp.

Stigmatochromis woodi is one of a few species of the Haplochromis group that does not possess blue pigment. Its primary coloration is metallic green and black. Pictured is a young male starting to develop spawning coloration.

Stigmatochromis sp. Guttatus is an extremely rare species that was recently collected for the first time. It bears a close resemblance to S. woodi. Pictured is a male collected near Liuli, Tanzania in deep water by Charles Kacirek.

Name: *Stigmatochromis woodi*
Location and Natural Habitat: Found throughout the lake from shallow water to a depth of at least 150 feet (45 m). Regularly inhabits the area where the sand and rocks intermingle.

Adult Size: To 8 inches (20 cm).

Husbandry Requirements: Best maintained in groups of six. Provide the aquarium with rocks piled up to form caves and passageways, and a thin layer of silica sand. Intolerant of poor water quality. Use no smaller than a 75-gallon (300 L) aquarium.

Diet: Small fishes and occasionally snails in the wild. Offer a high-protein diet of feeder guppies, fresh shrimp, chopped earthworms, and krill.

Breeding: The dominant male will construct a sand nest in which to spawn with any receptive female. After spawning, the female should be given enough hiding places to retire to for the duration of the brooding period. Feed juveniles live baby brine shrimp.

Name: *Stigmatochromis* sp. **Guttatus**
Location and Natural Habitat: Found throughout the lake over sandy areas. Most populations have been found in the southeast

Taeniochromis holotaenia is a predatory species and should not be maintained with any fish small enough for it to swallow.

The king of all Lake Malawi sand-dwelling cichlids is Taeniolethrinops praeorbitalis. *This large species requires an aquarium no smaller than 200 gallons. Pictured is a freshly captured male from Senga Bay.*

arm of the lake and along the Tanzanian coastline at Liuli. Inhabits depths from 80 to 330 feet (24–100 m).

Adult Size: To 7 inches (17.5 cm).

Husbandry Requirements: Provide the aquarium with a few rocks and a thin layer of silica sand. Intolerant of poor water quality. Use no smaller than a 75-gallon (300 L) aquarium.

Diet: Small sand-dwelling fishes. Feed a high-protein diet of feeder guppies, fresh shrimp, chopped earthworms, and krill.

Breeding: Has yet to be spawned in captivity due to insufficient numbers collected. Likely to be similar to its sister species, *Stigmatochromis woodi.*

Name: *Taeniochromis holotaenia*

Location and Natural Habitat: Found throughout the lake over sandy areas. Particularly common around the west side of Mbenji Island near the isthmus.

Adult Size: To 8 inches (20 cm).

Husbandry Requirements: A loosely schooling species. Maintain several together in an aquarium of at least 100 gallons (400 L). Provide a thin layer of silica sand and a few large, smooth stones.

Diet: Small fishes and invertebrates in the wild. Feed a high-protein diet of feeder guppies, fresh shrimp, chopped earthworms, and krill.

Breeding: The dominant male will construct a rudimentary sand nest and coax any receptive female to spawn. After spawning, the female will join with the other females to incubate her eggs. Feed newly released juveniles live baby brine shrimp and finely crushed flake foods.

Name: *Taeniolethrinops preaorbitalis*

Location and Natural Habitat: Found throughout the lake over sandy areas.

Adult Size: To 14 inches (42 cm).

Husbandry Requirements: A large species that will require a suitably large aquarium of at least 200 gallons (800 L). Provide most of the aquarium with a thin layer of silica sand. Best maintained with species that inhabit the upper water column such as any *Copadichromis* species.

Trematocranus placodon is sensitive to improper water quality. Large, frequent water changes will assure the health of this species.

Diet: Aquatic insect larvae in the sand in the wild. Feed a varied diet to include flakes, pellets, ocean plankton, krill, and frozen foods.

Breeding: If juveniles are purchased, it may take a couple of years for them to reach maturity. The dominant male will construct a large sand nest where spawning will take place. Females ready to spawn will enter the nest, while those not ready will be kept at bay. Afterwards, the brooding female will leave and join with other females. Feed juveniles live baby brine shrimp.

Name: *Trematocranus placodon*
Location and Natural Habitat: Found throughout the lake over sandy areas. Typically inhabits shallow water near beaches.

Adult Size: To 9 inches (22.5 cm).

Husbandry Requirements: Sensitive to improper water quality. Maintain over a sandy bottom, with a fine layer of silica sand. Best maintained with species that inhabit the upper water column such as any *Copadichromis* species. Aquarium should be at least 150 gallons (600 L).

Diet: Snails in the wild. Feed a high-protein diet to include fresh shrimp, aquatic snails, chopped earthworms, ocean plankton, and krill.

Breeding: The dominant male will construct a crater nest in the sand and coax any receptive female to spawn. After spawning, the brooding female will join with the other females. Feed live baby brine shrimp to newly released juveniles.

Name: *Tyrannochromis macrostoma*
Location and Natural Habitat: Found throughout the lake in areas with an even mixture of rocks and sand.

The large and predatory Tyrannochromis macrostoma *has proven itself to be an ideal aquarium resident, so long as it is maintained with similar-sized species. Pictured is a freshly captured male from Maleri Island.*

Adult Size: To 15 inches (45 cm).

Husbandry Requirements: A large, highly predatory species that should not be maintained with any other fishes small enough to fit into its mouth. Provide several large rocks piled up to form caves and passageways, and a fine layer of silica sand. Aquarium should be at least 200 gallons (800 L).

Diet: Fishes in the wild. Feed a high-protein diet consisting of live feeder guppies, fresh shrimp, ocean plankton, krill, and frozen aquarium foods.

Breeding: A large aquarium is a must to spawn this species successfully. The dominant male will stake out a large portion of the aquarium as his territory and spawning grounds. After spawning, provide the female with sufficient hiding places; otherwise, remove her to another aquarium so she may brood her eggs in peace. Feed juveniles live baby brine shrimp and finely crushed flake foods.

GLOSSARY

Anoxic: totally devoid of oxygen

Biotope: A living organism's natural habitat

Carnivore: flesh eating animal

Conspecifics: term applied to individuals of the same species

Cryptic: camouflage; an animal with a color pattern that mimics the color or shape of its habitat

Ctenoid scale: circular scale with several small pointed projections on its outer edge

Cycloid scale: circular scale with smooth edges all around

Herbivorous: plant eating animal

Heterotrophic bacteria: bacteria that are capable of using various organic materials for their food and energy needs

kH: carbonate hardness; the measurement of the amount of carbonate, or bicarbonate, in water

Lateral line: a series of receptors embedded in the scales of a fish that can usually be seen as a narrow line running horizontally down the body. These receptors enable the fish to detect movement in the water nearby

Mollusks: shelled invertebrates, such as snails and clams

Left: A small group of female **Melanochromis auratus** *from Masinje.*

Right: An adult female **Melanochromis johanni** *from Masinje.*

Pelagic: living in the open water away from the shoreline

pH: a value on a scale of 0 to 14 that indicates the acidity or alkalinity of water. Acidic water is less than 7, neutral water 7, and alkaline water higher than 7

Pharyngeal bones: bones located in the throat and studded with teeth that aid in the mastication of food

Phytoplankton: microscopic plants, usually algae, that float in the water

Piscivore, piscivorous: an animal that eats fish

Planktivorous: an animal that eats free-floating phytoplankton and zooplankton

Polyphyletic: A group of related organisms derived from several distinct ancestors

Zooplankton: tiny aquatic animals, usually crustacean and insect larvae, that float in the water

INFORMATION

Magazines

Tropical Fish Hobbyist
TFH Publications, Inc.
211 West Sylvania Avenue
Neptune, NJ 07753
908-988-8400

Aquarium Fish Magazine
Fancy Publications, Inc.
Subscription Department
P.O. Box 53351
Boulder, CO 80323-3351

Cichlid News
Aquatic Promotions, Inc.
P.O. Box 700166
Miami, FL 33170
305-247-0460

Journals

Ichthyological Explorations of Fresh Waters
Verlag Dr. Friedrich Pfiel
P.O. Box 65 00 86
D-81214, Munchen, Germany

Books

Demason, Laif. *A Guide To The Tanzanian Cichlids of Lake Malawi*. Ft. Myers, Florida: National Art Publishing, 1995.
Konings, Ad. *Book of Cichlids and All the Fishes of Lake Malawi*. Neptune, New Jersey: TFH Publications, Inc., 1989.
_____ . *Enjoying Cichlids*. St. Leon-Rot, Germany: Cichlid Press, 1993.
_____ . *Malawi Cichlids in Their Natural Habitat*, 2nd Edition. St. Leon-Rot, Germany: Cichlid Press, 1995.
_____ . *Back to Nature Guide to Malawi Cichlids*. Jonsered, Sweden: Fohrman Aquaristik AB, 1997.
Loiselle, Dr. Paul. *The Cichlid Aquarium*. Blacksburg, Virginia: Tetra Press, 1994.
Schraml, Erwin (Editor). *African Cichlids 1 (Malawi, Mbuna)*. Walldorf, Germany: Verlag A.C.S. GmbH, 1998.
_____ . *African Cichlids 2 (Malawi)*. Walldorf, Germany: Verlag A.C.S. GmbH, 2000.
Spreinat, Andreas. *Lake Malawi Cichlids from Tanzania*. Gottingen, Germany: Verduijn Cichlids, 1995.

Book Dealers

Aquatic Book Shop
P.O. Box 2150
Shingle Springs, CA 95682-2150
530-622-7157

Cichlid Press
4170 Valplano Drive
El Paso, TX 79912

Aquatic Promotions, Inc.
P.O. Box 700166
Miami, FL 33170
Tel/Fax: 305-247-0460

Internet Sites

Aquatic Book Shop   *http://www.seahorses.com*
Cichlid Press   *http://www.cichlidpress.com*
The Cichlid Room Companion *http://www.petsforum.com/cichlidroom/default.html*

One of the more popular color variants of **Aulonocara stuartgranti** *is this specimen from Usisya.*

National Cichlid Clubs

American Cichlid Association
524 Prairie Knoll Drive
Naperville, IL 60565

Pacific Coast Cichlid Association
P.O. Box 28145
San Jose, CA 95128

Greater Chicago Cichlid Association
41 West 510 Route 20
Hampshire, IL 60140

International Cichlid Clubs

Germany
Deutsche Cichliden Gesellschaft
Parkstrasse 21a
D-33719 Bielfeld

England
British Cichlid Association
248 Longridge, Knutsford
Cheshire, WA18 8PH

France
Association France Cichlid
15 Rue des Hirondelles
f-67350 Daunendorf

Netherlands
Nederlandse Cichliden Vereniging
Boeier 31
NL-1625 CJ Hoorn

Important Note
Electrical equipment for aquarium care is described in this book. Please do not fail to read the note below, since otherwise serious accidents could occur.

Water damage from broken glass, overflowing, or tank leaks cannot always be avoided. Therefore, you should not fail to take out insurance.

Please take special care that neither children nor adults ever eat any aquarium plants. It can cause serious health injury. Fish medication should be kept away from children.

Safety Around the Aquarium
Water and electricity can lead to dangerous accidents. Therefore, you should make absolutely sure when buying equipment that it is suitable for use in an aquarium.
✔ Every technical device must have the UL sticker on it. These letters give the assurance that the safety of the equipment has been carefully checked by experts and that "with ordinary use" (as the experts say) nothing dangerous can happen.
✔ Always unplug any electrical equipment before you do any cleaning around or in the aquarium.
✔ Never do your own repairs on the aquarium or the equipment if there is something wrong with it. As a matter of safety, all repairs should only be carried out by an expert.

Aquarium:
adding new Cichlids to, 31
decorations for, 20–21
filtration of, 16–18, 22–23
heater and thermometer for, 19–20
lighting for, 20
live plants for, 21
sand/gravel for, 21
size and shape, 15–16
stand for, 16
water changes, 25–26
water chemistry, 19
Aristochromis christyi, **9**, 63, **63**
Aulonocara:
hansbaenschi, **12**, **63**, 63–64
jacobfreibergi, **14**, **20**, **64**, 65
sp. Maleri, **65**, 65–66
stuartgranti, **64**, 64–65

Baby brine shrimp, raising, 36–37
Bacterial infections, 27–30
Bloat, 29
Buccochromis rhoadesii, 66, **66**

Champsochromis:
caeruleus, **66**, 66–67
spilorynchus, 67, **67**
Chilotilapia rhoadesii, **67**, 67–68
Cichlids:
anatomy, **11**, 13
diet of, 7–8, 27
diversity of, 5–6
features of, 12–13
flock size, 8–9
spawning tips for, 33–39
water type and habitat for, 6–7
Copadichromis:
azureus, 68, **68**
borleyi, **9**, **68**, 68–69
trewavasae, 69, **69**
verduyni, **69**, 69–70
virginalis, **31**, 70, **70**
Crytocara moorii, **70**, 70–71
Cynotilapia afra, **11**, **20**, **40**, 41, **42**

Diet, 7–8, 27
Dimidiochromis:
compressiceps, 71, **71**
strigatus, **71**, 71–72
Diplotaxodon ecclesi, **35**

Eclectochromis:
milomo, 72, **72**
sp. Mbenji Thick Lips, **72**, 72–73
Exochochromis anagenys, 73, **73**

Filtration, 16–18, 22–23

Genyochromis mento, **42**, 42–43

Haplochromines, 5–7, 63–89
Hole-in-the-head, 29–30
Hospital aquarium, 30

Ichthyophthirius, 28
Iodotropheus sprengerae, 43, **43**

Labeotropheus:
fuelleborni, 43–44, **43–44**
trewavasae, **40**, **44**, 44–45
Labidochromis:
caeruleus, 45, **45**
sp. Mbamba Bay, **45**, 45–46
sp. Perlmutt, 46, **46**
Lake Malawi:
facts about, 12
history, 9–11
layers of, 6–7
Lethrinops:
cf. lethrinus, **73**, 73–74
sp. Nyassae, 74, **74**
Lichnochromis acuticeps, 74, **74**

Mbuna group, 42–63
Melanochromis:
auratus, 46, **47**
baliodigma, 47, **47**
johannii, **18**, 47–48, **48**
labrosus, 48, **48**
lepidiadaptes, 48–49, **49**
vermivorus, 49, **49**
Metriaclima:
aurora, **14**, 49, 49–50

barlowi, 50, **50**
callainos, **50**, 50–51
crabro, 51, **51**
estherae, **31**, **35**, **51**, 51–52
lombardoi, 52, **52**
mbenjii, **24**, 52–53, **53**
pyrsonotus, **53**, 53–54
zebra, **19**, **31**, 54, **54**
Mouthbrooders, 5–6
Mylochromis:
gracilis, 75, **75**
sp. Lateristriga Makanjila, 75, **75**

Nimbochromis:
fuscotaeniatus, 75–76, **76**
linni, **8**, 76, **76**
livingstonii, **9**, 77, **77**
polystigma, **37**, 77, **77**
venustus, **30**, 77–78, **78**

"Otopharynx":
sp. Silver Torpedo, 79–80, **80**
Otopharynx:
lithobates, **7**, **35**, 78, **78**
sp. Blue Otter, 79, **79**
walteri, 78–79, **79**

Parasites, 27–30
Petrotilapia:
chrysos, **54**, 54–55
sp. Small Blue, 55, **55**
Placidochromis:
electra, 80, **80**
phenochilus, 80–81, **81**
sp. Johnstoni Solo, 81, **81**
Protomelas:
annectens, 81–82, **82**
cf. taeniolatus, **21**, **35**, 84–85, **85**
dejunctus, 82, **82**
fenestratus, 83, **83**
marginatus, 82–83, **83**
sp. Spilonotus Tanzania, 83–84, **84**
sp. Steveni Taiwan, 84, **84**
Pseudotropheus:
cyaneus, **55**, 55–56
demasoni, 56, **56**
flavus, 56, **56**
saulosi, **8**, 57, **57**
socolofi, **57**, 57–58

sp. Acei, 58, **58**
sp. Chewere Elongatus, **58**, 58–59
sp. Masimbwe Elongatus, **29**, 59, **59**
sp. Msobo, **59**, 59–60
sp. Red Top Ndumbi, 60, **60**

Quarantine, 30

Rhamphochromis cf. macrophthalmus, 85, **85**

Sciaenochromis fryeri, 86, **86**
Spawning:
difficult-to-spawn species, 34–35
habitats for, 33–34
inbreeding, avoiding, 33
juveniles
foods for, 36–37
separating from parents, 38–39
preparing for, 33
Stigmatochromis:
modestus, 86, **86**
sp. Guttatus, **87**, 87–88
woodi, 87, **87**
Substrate spawners, 5–6

Taeniochromis holotaenia, **87**, 88
Taeniolethrinops preaorbitalis, **88**, 88–89
Test kits, 25–26
Tilapiines, 5–7
Trematocranus placodon, **88**, 89
Tropheops:
gracilior, **60**, 60–61
sp. Chitande Yellow, **61**, 61–62
sp. Red Cheek, 62, **62**
sp. Red Fin, **62**, 62–63
tropheops, 61, **61**
Tyrannochromis macrostoma, **32**, 89, **89**

Water:
changes, 25–26
chemistry, 19
pH of, 19

Dedication

To my parents, David and Harriet Smith, who have instructed me to see the truth of Psalm 19 and Romans 1:20–23.

Acknowledgments

The author wishes to thank the following people who have, over the years, offered their unyielding hospitality and access to their fishes to photograph. Many have given of their time to help me to understand various perplexing concepts and ideas. Thanks to such people for their patience with my seemingly endless bombardment of questions, theories, and ideas. My deepest apologies if I have inadvertently omitted those who figured significantly in my evolving knowledge of the cichlids of Lake Malawi.

I would like to make special mention of Stuart Grant of Lake Malawi Cichlid Center, Salima, Malawi for his generous hospitality during expeditions to the lake in 1990, 1991, and 1993. Without his help and that of his assistants, boats, and diving equipment, my trips to the lake would have been in vain.

I would also like to thank the following people for their mutual interests in the cichlids of Lake Malawi and for the offering up of their ideas, as well as those who have graciously given me access to their Malawi cichlids for photographing purposes: Jurg Bahler, Mary Bailey, Dr. George Barlow, John Benson, Rich and Laura Birley, Dr. Warren Burgess, Ron Coleman, Laif Demason, Phil Farrel, Lee Finley, Kjell Fohrman, Jim and Agnus Forshey, Robert Gillespie, Tim Hovanec, Ray Hunziker, Charles Kacirek, Ad Konings, Yiu Hung Li, Dr. Paul Loiselle, John Lombardo, Steve Lundblad, John Niemans, Art North, Dr. Michel Oliver, Ralph Paccione, Michel and Clotilde Perbost, Harry Piken, Chuck Rambo, Robert Rodriquez, Ben Rosler, Harold Scheel, Delores Schehr, David Schleser, Ron Sousy, Dick Strever, Stan Sung, and Jerry Walls.

Photo Credits

All photos are by the author.

Cover Photos

The author: front cover, back cover, inside front cover, inside back cover.

About the Author

Mark Phillip Smith is a professional wildlife photographer, explorer, and discoverer of freshwater temperate and tropical fishes. In 1990, he contributed to the discovery of a genus and two species of Lake Malawi cichlids. In 1994, he discovered several new species of cichlids in Lake Edward, Uganda. His ichthyological interests have taken him to Japan, Mexico, Uruguay, Malawi, Zambia, Argentina, Zimbabwe, Kenya, Uganda, England, Sweden, Hawaii, and the Caribbean. He writes for domestic and international publications, and lectures widely on the cichlids of Lake Tanganyika and Lake Malawi.

All inquiries should be addressed to:
Barron's Educational Series, Inc.
250 Wireless Boulevard
Hauppauge, NY 11788
http://www.barronseduc.com

International Standard Book No. 0-7641-1525-1

Library of Congress Catalog Card No. 00-036279

Library of Congress Cataloging-in-Publication Data
Smith, Mark Phillip, 1966–
    Lake Malawi Cichlids : a complete pet owner's manual : everything about history, setting up an aquarium, health concerns, and spawning / Mark Smith.
        p. cm. – (A complete pet owner's manual)
    Includes bibliographical references (p.   ).
    ISBN 0-7641-1525-1 (pbk.)
    1. Cichlids—Nyasa, Lake. 2. Aquarium fishes.
I. Title. II. Series.
SF458.C5 S53   2000
639.3'774—dc21   00-036279

Printed in Hong Kong
9 8 7 6 5 4 3 2 1